CAREERS FOR

PERSUASIVE
TYPES

& Others Who Won't Take No for an Answer

W9-BNA-230

CAREERS FOR

PERSUASIVE TYPES

& Others Who Won't Take No for an Answer

Jan Goldberg

VGM Career Horizons
NTC/Contemporary Publishing Group

Library of Congress Cataloging-in-Publication Data

Goldberg, Jan.
    Careers for persuasive types & others who won't take no for an answer / Jan
Goldberg.
       p.   cm. — (VGM careers for you series)
      ISBN 0-658-00217-1 — ISBN 0-658-00218-X (pb)
      1. Vocational guidance. 2. Oral communication. 3. Persuasion (Psychology) 4.
Negotiation in business.   I. Title: Careers for persuasive types and others who
won't take no for an answer.   II. Title.   III. Series.
HF5381.G56824   2000
331.7′02—dc21

                                                           99–56607
                                                               CIP

Published by VGM Career Horizons
A division of NTC/Contemporary Publishing Group, Inc.
4255 West Touhy Avenue, Lincolnwood (Chicago), Illinois 60712-1975 U.S.A.
Copyright © 2000 by NTC/Contemporary Publishing Group, Inc.
Printed in the United States of America
International Standard Book Number: 0-658-00217-1 (cloth)
                                        0-658-00218-X (paper)
00 01 02 03 04 05 LB 18 17 16 15 14 13 12 11 10 9 8 7 6 5 4 3 2 1

To the memory of my beloved
parents, Sam and Sylvia
Lefkovitz, and the memory of a
dear uncle, Bernard Lefko.

Contents

Acknowledgments

The author gratefully acknowledges:

- The numerous professionals who graciously agreed to be profiled in this book

- My dear husband, Larry, for his inspiration and vision

- My children—Sherri, Deborah, and Bruce—for their encouragement and love

- Family and close friends—Adrienne, Marty, Mindi, Cary, Michele, Paul, Michele, Alison, Steve, Marci, Steve, Brian, Steven, Jesse, Colin, Andrew, Bertha, and Aunt Helen—for their kindness and support

- Diana Catlin, for her insights and input

- Betsy Lancefield, editor at VGM, for making all projects rewarding and enjoyable

Introduction

By persuading others, we convince ourselves.   JUNIUS

Webster defines the word *persuade* in the following manner: *induce belief in; convince.* What personal qualities make someone persuasive? Are you the kind of person whom others find to be persuasive? Do you think you are a persuasive person? Take the following true-or-false quiz, and you'll find out! It just might provide some valuable insight into your personality!

Persuasiveness Quiz

1. I am able to think of several different ways to present a project or an idea.

2. I am usually able to make other people see a problem (challenge) my way.

3. I enjoy new experiences.

4. New challenges excite me.

5. I trust my intuition.

6. I continue on with a project or idea even though most people would have given up.

7. I find it easy to talk with complete strangers.

8. I avoid thinking in terms of success and failure.

9. I try to get to know as many people as possible in social situations.

10. Even in a new environment, I have no problem making contacts quickly.

11. People tend to remember me, even after only one contact.

12. I have a good memory for names, faces, and details.

13. I am an outgoing person.

14. I am able to think logically.

15. I am good at solving problems.

16. I am a good listener.

17. I am able to organize my thoughts effectively.

18. I am self-confident.

19. I am able to adjust my approach to the situation at hand.

20. I am a gregarious person.

21. I follow through on projects.

22. People like me.

23. I am a goal-oriented person.

24. I read profusely.

25. I strive for success, both for myself and for those with whom I interact.

If most of your responses were true, you may indeed be a persuasive person. If so, you might seriously want to consider exploring some of the careers highlighted in this book. All of them—sales, advertising, marketing, public relations, fund-raising, politics, law, and education—particularly lend themselves to success for those individuals who have persuasive personalities.

One of our most well-known presidents had an interesting view on the concept of persuasion:

I sit here all day trying to persuade people to do the things they ought to have sense enough to do without my persuading them. That's all the powers of the president amount to. HARRY S. TRUMAN

CHAPTER ONE

Careers in Sales

[A salesman is] an optimist who finds the world full of promising potential. JERRY DASHKIN

The field of sales encompasses a wide range of job settings, products, and services, as well as methods of selling. Here's a sample advertisement that captures some of the elements of a career in sales.

HELP WANTED: RETAIL SALES

If you enjoy art and design, work well with people, and are looking for an interesting and challenging full-time job, we have the ideal position in our art gallery. Your schedule will include Saturday hours from 10 A.M. until 6 P.M. and Sunday noon until 5 P.M. Compensation will depend upon applicant's qualifications. If you are interested, please contact us immediately.

Sales careers can be broken into the following three primary categories:

Retail

Services

Manufacturing and Wholesale

Several other sales categories do not exactly fit into those three and have carved their own niches. They include insurance sales, real estate sales, and travel agents.

Retail Sales Workers

Every day, millions of dollars are spent on a wide variety of merchandise—everything from sweaters and hats to mattresses and furniture. No matter what the item, a sales worker's primary job is to interest customers in the merchandise. Aids in this process include describing the product's features, demonstrating its use, showing various models and colors, and pointing out why products will benefit the customer or client.

For some jobs, particularly those involving the selling of expensive and complex items, special knowledge or skills are needed. For example, workers who sell personal computers must be able to explain to customers the features of various brands and models, the meaning of manufacturers' specifications, and the types of software that are available.

In other jobs, selling standardized articles such as food, hardware, linens, and housewares, sales workers may often do little more than take payments and bag purchases.

Some retail sales workers also receive cash, check, and charge payments; handle returns; and give change and receipts. Depending on the hours they work, they may have to open or close the cash register. This may include counting the money in the cash register; separating charge slips, coupons, and exchange vouchers; and making deposits at the cash office. Sales workers are often held responsible for the contents of their registers, and, in many organizations, repeated shortages are cause for dismissal.

In addition, sales workers may help stock shelves or racks, arrange for mailing or delivery of a purchase, mark price tags, take inventory, and prepare displays.

Sales workers must be aware of not only the promotions their stores are sponsoring but also those that are being sponsored by competitors. Also, they often must recognize potential security risks and know how to handle such situations.

Consumers often form their impressions of a store by its sales force. The retail industry is very competitive, and, increasingly, employers are stressing the importance of providing courteous and efficient service. When a customer wants a product that is not on the sales floor, for example, the sales worker may check the stockroom and, if there are none in stock, place a special order or call another store to locate the item.

Job Settings

The largest employers of retail sales workers are department stores. Other types of employers include specialty shops, boutiques, independently owned stores, and large chain outlets, such as those selling hardware or office supplies.

Catalog and on-line sales are two large areas that provide additional avenues for those interested in venturing into sales as a career. In fact, the on-line sales market continues to broaden and deepen, with more products and services available on-line taking a bigger and bigger share of the total sales market.

Telemarketing is another huge industry. Everything from time-share vacations to telephone service to credit cards are solicited by phone.

Qualifications and Training

Usually, there are no formal education requirements for this type of work. Employers look for candidates who enjoy working with people and have the tact and patience to deal with difficult customers. Among other desirable characteristics are an interest in sales work, a neat appearance, and the ability to communicate clearly and effectively.

Before hiring, some employers may conduct a background check, especially for jobs in selling high-priced items. In most small stores, an experienced employee or the proprietor instructs newly hired sales personnel in making out sales checks and operating the cash register. In larger stores, training programs are more formal and are usually conducted over several days.

As salespeople gain experience and seniority, they usually move to positions of greater responsibility and are given their choices of departments. This often means moving to areas with potentially higher earnings and commissions. The highest earning potential is usually found in selling big-ticket items. This work often requires the most knowledge of the product and the greatest talent for persuasion.

In years past, capable sales workers without college degrees could advance to management positions, but today, large retail businesses generally prefer to hire college graduates as management trainees. This makes a college education increasingly important. Despite this trend, capable employees without college degrees should still be able to advance to administrative or supervisory work in large stores.

Opportunities for advancement vary in small stores. In some establishments, advancement opportunities are limited because one person, often the owner, does most of the managerial work. In others, however, some sales workers can be promoted to assistant managers.

Retail selling experience may be an asset when applying for sales positions with larger retailers or in other industries, such as financial services, wholesale trade, or manufacturing.

Salaries

The starting salary for many part-time retail sales positions is the federal minimum wage. In some areas where employers are having difficulty attracting and retaining workers, wages are much higher than the established minimum.

The following list shows average weekly earnings by class of sales worker in several industries.

Motor vehicle and boats—$593

Radio, television, hi-fi, and appliances—$423

Furniture and home furnishings—$403

Hardware and building supplies—$372

Parts—$409

Apparel—$265

Shoes —$328

Compensation systems vary by type of establishment and merchandise sold. Some sales workers receive an hourly wage. Others receive a commission or a combination of wages and commissions. Under a commission system, salespeople receive a percentage of the sales they make. These systems offer sales workers the opportunity to significantly increase their earnings, but they may find their earnings depend on both their ability to sell their products and the ups and downs in the economy.

In addition, nearly all sales workers are able to buy store merchandise at a discount, often from 10 to 40 percent below regular prices. In some cases, this privilege is extended to the employee's family as well.

Services Sales Representatives

Services sales representatives sell a wide variety of services. For example, sales representatives for data processing services firms sell complex services such as inventory control, payroll processing, sales analysis, and financial reporting systems. Hotel sales representatives contact government, business, and social groups to solicit convention and conference business for the hotel. Fund-raisers plan programs to raise money for charities or other nonprofit causes. Sales representatives for temporary help services firms locate and acquire clients who will hire the firm's employees.

Telephone services sales representatives visit commercial customers to review their telephone systems, analyze their communications needs, and recommend services such as installation of additional equipment. Other representatives sell automotive leasing, public utility, burial, shipping, protective, and management consulting services.

Services sales representatives act as industry experts, consultants, and problem solvers when selling their firms' services. The sales representative, in some cases, creates demand for his or her firm's services. A prospective client who is asked to consider buying a particular service may never have used, or have even been aware of a need for, that service. For example, wholesalers might be persuaded to order a list of credit ratings for checking their customers' credit prior to making sales and discover that the list could be used to solicit new business.

There are several different categories of services sales jobs, including outside and inside sales and telemarketing. *Outside sales representatives* call on clients and prospects at their homes or offices. They may have an appointment, or they may practice cold calls, arriving without an appointment. *Inside sales representatives* work on their employers' premises, assisting individuals interested in the company's services. *Telemarketing sales representatives* sell exclusively over the telephone. They make large numbers of calls to prospects, attempting to sell the company's service themselves or to arrange an appointment between the prospect and an outside sales representative. Some sales representatives deal exclusively with one, or a few, major clients.

Despite the diversity of services being sold, the jobs of all services sales representatives have much in common. All sales representatives must fully understand and be able to discuss the services their companies offer.

Also, the procedures they follow are similar. Many sales representatives develop lists of prospective clients through telephone and business directories, asking business associates and customers for leads, and calling on new businesses as they cover their assigned territories. Some services sales reps acquire clients through inquiries about the company's services.

Regardless of how they first meet the client, all services sales representatives must explain how the services being offered can meet the client's needs. This often involves demonstrations of the company's services. Sales reps must answer questions about the nature and cost of the services and try to overcome objections in order to persuade potential customers to purchase the services. If they fail to make a sale on the first visit, they may follow up with more visits, letters, or phone calls. After closing a sale, services sales representatives generally follow up to see that the purchase meets the customer's needs and to determine whether additional services can be sold.

Because services sales representatives obtain many of their new accounts through referrals, success hinges on developing a satisfied clientele who will continue to use the services and will recommend them to other potential customers. Like other types of sales jobs, a services sales representative's reputation is crucial to his or her success.

Services sales work varies with the kind of service sold. Selling highly technical services, such as communications systems or computer consulting, involves complex and lengthy sales negotiations. In addition, sales of complex services may require extensive after-sale support. In these situations, sales representatives may operate as part of a team of sales representatives and experts from other departments. Sales representatives receive valuable technical assistance from these experts. For example, those who sell data processing services might work with a systems engineer or computer scientist, and those who sell telephone services might receive technical assistance from a communications consultant. Teams enhance customer service and build strong long-term relationships with customers, resulting in increased sales.

Because of the length of time between the initial contact with a customer and the actual sale, representatives who sell complex technical services generally work with several customers simultaneously. Sales representatives must be well organized and efficient in scheduling their time.

Selling less complex services, such as linen supply or exterminating services, generally involves simpler and shorter sales negotiations. A sales representative's job may likewise vary with the size of the employer. Those working for large companies generally are more specialized and are assigned territorial boundaries, a specific line of services, and their own accounts. In smaller companies, sales representatives may have broader responsibilities—administration, marketing, public relations—in addition to their sales duties.

Job Settings

Services sales representatives hold more than five hundred thousand jobs nationwide. More than half of these jobs are in firms providing business services, including computer and data processing, advertising, personnel supply, equipment rental and leasing, and mailing, reproduction, and stenographic services.

Other sales representatives work for firms that offer a wide range of other services, such as business services (advertising, computer and data processing, personnel supply, mailing), engineering and management, personal, amusement and recreation, automotive repair, membership organizations, hotels, motion pictures, health, and education.

Qualifications and Training

Many employers require services sales representatives to have college degrees, but requirements may vary depending on the industry a particular company represents. Employers who market advertising services seek individuals with degrees in advertising or marketing or master's degrees in business administration; companies that market educational services prefer individuals with advanced degrees in marketing or related fields.

Many hotels seek graduates from college hotel administration programs, and companies that sell computer services and telephone systems prefer sales representatives with a background in computer science or engineering. College courses in business, economics, communications, and marketing are helpful in obtaining other jobs as services sales representatives.

Employers may hire experienced, high-performing sales representatives who have only a high school diploma. This is particularly true for those who sell nontechnical services, such as exterminating, laundry, or funeral services.

Many firms conduct intensive training programs for their sales representatives. A sound training program covers the history of the business; origin, development, and uses of the service; effective prospecting methods; and presentation of the service. Training also covers answering customer objections, creating customer demand, closing a sale, writing an order, understanding company policies, and consulting with and coordinating the services of technical support personnel.

Services sales representatives may also attend seminars on a wide range of subjects given by in-house or outside training institutions. These sessions acquaint employees with new services and products and help them maintain and update their sales techniques. Such sessions may also include motivational or sensitivity training to make sales representatives more effective in dealing with people. Sales workers generally receive training in the use of computers and communications technology in order to increase their productivity.

In order to be successful, sales representatives should have a pleasant, outgoing personality and good rapport with people. They must be highly motivated, well organized, and efficient. Good grooming and a neat appearance are essential, as are self-confidence, reliability, and the ability to effectively communicate. Sales representatives should be self-starters who have the ability to work under pressure to meet sales goals.

Sales representatives who have good sales records and leadership abilities may advance to supervisory and managerial positions. Frequent contact with businesspeople in other firms provides sales workers with leads about job openings and enhances advancement opportunities.

Salaries

The median annual income for full-time advertising sales representatives is about $26,000. Representatives selling other types of business services earn about $30,200. Earnings of representatives who sell technical services generally are higher than earnings of those who sell nontechnical services.

The average yearly income for entry-level sales is about $36,000, ranging up to $63,000 for senior sales staff.

Earnings of experienced sales representatives depend on performance. Successful sales representatives who establish a strong customer base can earn more than managers in their firms. Some sales representatives earn well over $100,000 a year.

Sales representatives work on different types of compensation plans. Some get a straight salary; others are paid solely on a commission basis—a percentage of the dollar value of their sales. Most firms use a combination of salary and commissions. Some services sales representatives receive a base salary plus incentive pay that adds 50 to 70 percent to the sales representative's base salary. In addition to the same benefits package received by other employees of the firm, outside sales representatives have expense accounts to cover meals and travel, and some drive a company car. Many employers offer bonuses—including vacation time, trips, and prizes—for sales that exceed company quotas.

In spite of all the perks, with fluctuating economic conditions and consumer and business expectations, earnings may vary widely from year to year.

Manufacturers' and Wholesale Sales Representatives and Sales Managers

Articles of clothing, books, and computers are among the thousands of products bought and sold each day. Manufacturers' and wholesale sales representatives play an important role in this process. While retail sales workers sell products directly to customers, manufacturers' representatives market the company's products to other manufacturers, wholesale and retail establishments, government agencies, and other institutions. Regardless of the type of products they sell, the primary duties of these sales representatives are to interest wholesale and retail buyers and purchasing agents in their merchandise and ensure that any questions or concerns of current clients are addressed. Sales reps also provide advice to clients on how to increase sales.

Depending on where they work, these sales representatives have different job titles. Many of those representing manufacturers are referred to as manufacturers' representatives, and those employed by wholesalers generally are called sales representatives. Those selling technical products, for both manufacturers and wholesalers, are usually called industrial sales workers or sales engineers. In addition to those employed directly by firms, manufacturers' agents are self-employed sales workers who contract their services to all types of companies.

Manufacturers' and wholesale sales representatives spend much of their time traveling to and visiting with prospective buyers and current clients. During sales calls, they discuss the customers' needs and suggest how their merchandise or services can meet those needs. They may show samples or catalogs that describe items the company stocks and inform customers about prices, availability, and how their products can save money and improve productivity. In addition, because of the vast number of manufacturers and wholesalers selling similar products, they try to beat the competition by emphasizing the unique qualities of the products and services offered by their companies. They also take orders and resolve any problems or complaints with the merchandise.

These sales representatives have additional duties as well. For example, sales engineers, who are among the most highly trained sales workers, typically sell products whose installation and optimal use require technical expertise and support products such as material handling equipment, numerical-control machinery, and computer systems.

In addition to providing information on their firms' products, these workers help prospective and current buyers with technical problems. For example, they may recommend improved materials and machinery for a firm's manufacturing process, draw up plans of proposed machinery layouts, and estimate cost savings from the use of their equipment. They present this information and negotiate the sale, a process that may take several months.

Sales engineers must also provide follow-up services, keeping close contact with the client to assure the client renews the contract. Sales engineers may work with engineers in their own companies, adapting products to a customer's special needs.

Increasingly, sales representatives who lack technical expertise work as a team with a technical expert. For example, a sales representative will make the preliminary contact with customers, introduce his or her company's product, and close the sale. However, the technically trained person will attend the sales presentation to explain and answer technical questions and concerns. In this way, the sales representative is able to spend more time maintaining and soliciting accounts and less time acquiring technical knowledge.

Obtaining new accounts is an important part of the job. Sales representatives follow leads suggested by other clients, from advertisements in trade journals, and from participation in trade shows and conferences. At times, they make unannounced visits to potential clients. In addition, they may spend a lot of time meeting with and entertaining prospective clients during evenings and weekends.

The daily activities of sales reps are tracked by supervisors— where they have been, who they have seen, and what they have sold. Sales representatives also analyze sales statistics, prepare reports, and handle administrative duties, such as filing expense account reports, scheduling appointments, and making travel plans. They study literature about new and existing products and monitor the sales, prices, and products of their competitors.

In addition to all these duties, manufacturers' agents must manage their own businesses. As agents, they often represent several manufacturers, which requires excellent organizational skills as well as knowledge of accounting, marketing, and, if hiring assistants, management and administration.

Some manufacturers' and wholesale sales representatives have large territories and do considerable traveling. Because a sales region may cover several states, they may be away from home for several days or weeks at a time. Others work near their home bases and do most of their traveling by automobile. Because of the nature of the work and the amount of travel, sales representatives typically work more than forty hours per week.

Sales managers direct corporate sales programs. They assign sales territories and goals and establish training programs for their sales representatives. Managers advise their sales representatives on ways to improve sales performance. In large, multi-product firms, they oversee regional and local sales managers and their staff members. Sales managers maintain contact with dealers and distributors. They analyze sales statistics gathered by their staff members to determine sales potential and inventory requirements and monitor the preferences of customers. Such information is vital to develop products and maximize profits.

Sales managers also have to go out in the field to see their sales reps. They make sure the reps are using the right techniques and handling each situation the way it should be handled in order to get the maximum sales volume. The reps can't afford to take the time to come to the office and lose sales.

Qualifications and Training

The background needed for sales jobs varies by product line and market. As the number of college graduates has increased and the job requirements have become more technical and analytical, most firms have placed a greater emphasis on a strong educational background. Nevertheless, many employers still hire individuals with previous sales experience who do not have college degrees. In fact, for some consumer products, sales ability, personality, and familiarity with brands are more important than a degree.

On the other hand, firms selling industrial products often require degrees in science or engineering in addition to some sales experience. In general, companies are looking for the best and brightest individuals who display an outgoing personality and the desire to sell.

Many companies have formal training programs for beginning sales reps that last up to two years. However, most businesses are accelerating these programs to reduce costs and expedite the return from training. In some programs, trainees rotate among jobs in plants and offices to learn all phases of product production, installation, and distribution. In others, trainees take formal classroom instruction at the plant, followed by on-the-job training under the supervision of a field sales manager.

In some firms, new workers are trained by accompanying more experienced workers on their sales calls. As these workers gain familiarity with the firm's products and clients, they are given increasing responsibility until they are eventually assigned their own territories. As businesses experience greater competition, increased pressure is placed upon sales representatives to produce faster.

These workers must stay abreast of new merchandise and the changing needs of their customers. They may attend trade shows where new products are displayed or conferences and conventions where they meet with other sales representatives and clients to discuss new product developments. In addition, many companies sponsor meetings of the entire sales force at which presentations are made on sales performance, product development, and profitability.

Sales representatives should enjoy traveling because much of their time is spent visiting current and prospective clients.

Salaries

Compensation methods vary significantly by the type of firm and product sold. However, most employers use a combination of salary and commission or salary plus bonus. Commissions are usually based on the amount of sales, whereas bonuses may depend on individual performance, on the performance of all sales workers in the group or district, or on the company's performance as a whole.

Median annual earnings of full-time manufacturers' and wholesale sales representatives is about $36,000, although some might start out as low as $16,000 and range up to $62,000 or more per year. Earnings vary by experience and the type of goods or services sold.

In addition to their earnings, sales representatives are usually reimbursed for expenses such as transportation costs, meals, hotels, and entertaining customers. They often receive benefits such as health and life insurance, a pension plan, vacation and sick leave, personal use of a company car, and frequent flyer mileage. Some companies offer incentives such as free vacation trips or gifts for outstanding sales workers.

Unlike those working directly for a manufacturer or wholesaler, manufacturers' agents work strictly on commission. Depending on the types of products they are selling, their experience in the field, and the number of clients, their earnings can be significantly higher or lower than those working in direct sales. In addition, because manufacturers' agents are self-employed, they must pay their own travel and entertainment expenses as well as provide for their own benefits, which can be a significant cost. Frequently, promotion takes the form of an assignment to a larger account or territory where commissions are likely to be greater. Experienced sales representatives may move into jobs as sales trainers who train new employees on selling techniques and company policies and procedures. Those who have good sales records and leadership ability may advance to sales supervisors or district managers.

In addition to advancement opportunities within a firm, some go into business for themselves as manufacturers' agents. Others find opportunities in buying, purchasing, advertising, or marketing research. For many sales reps, the end goal is to climb the ladder in sales and transfer into marketing.

Insurance Sales

Insurance agents and brokers sell insurance policies to individuals and businesses, providing protection against financial loss. Policies cover health, life, automobiles, jewelry, personal valuables, furniture, household items, businesses, real estate, and other properties.

Agents and brokers prepare reports, maintain records, and, in the event of a loss, help policyholders settle insurance claims. Specialists in group policies may help an employer provide employees with the opportunity to buy insurance through payroll deductions. Insurance agents may work for one insurance company or as independent agents selling for several companies. Insurance brokers do not sell for a particular company but place insurance policies for their clients with the company that offers the best rate and coverage.

Life insurance agents and brokers also are sometimes called *life underwriters*. Property/casualty insurance agents and brokers sell policies that protect individuals and businesses from financial loss as a result of automobile accidents, fire or theft, or other property losses. Property/casualty insurance can also cover workers' compensation, product liability, or medical malpractice. Many life and property/casualty insurance agents also sell health insurance policies covering the costs of hospital and medical care or loss of income due to illness or injury.

Because insurance sales agents obtain many new accounts through referrals, it is important that agents maintain regular contact with their clients to ensure their financial needs are being met as personal and business needs change. Developing a satisfied clientele who will recommend an agent's services to other potential customers is a key to success in this field.

Training

For jobs selling insurance, companies prefer college graduates, particularly those who have majored in business or economics. Some hire high school graduates with potential or proven sales ability or who have been successful in other types of work. In fact, most entrants to agent and broker jobs transfer from other occupations, so they tend to be older, on average, than entrants to many other occupations.

Many colleges and universities offer courses in insurance, and some schools offer bachelor's degrees in insurance. College courses in finance, mathematics, accounting, economics, business law, government, and business administration enable insurance agents or brokers to understand how social, marketing, and economic conditions relate to the insurance industry.

It is important for insurance agents and brokers to stay current with issues concerning clients. Changes in tax laws, government benefit programs, and other state and federal regulations can affect the insurance needs of clients and how agents conduct business. Courses in psychology, sociology, and public speaking can prove useful in improving sales techniques.

In addition, some basic familiarity with computers is very important. The use of computers to provide instantaneous information on a wide variety of financial products has greatly improved agents' and brokers' efficiency and enabled them to devote more time to clients.

All insurance agents and brokers must obtain a license in the states in which they plan to sell insurance. In most states, licenses are issued only to applicants who complete specified courses and then pass written examinations covering insurance fundamentals and the state insurance laws.

New agents usually receive training at the agencies where they work and, frequently, also at the insurance company's home office. Beginners sometimes attend company-sponsored classes to prepare for examinations. Others study on their own and accompany experienced agents when they call on prospective clients.

Insurance agents and brokers need to be enthusiastic, outgoing, self-confident, disciplined, hard working, and able to communicate effectively. They should be able to inspire customer confidence. Some companies give personality tests to prospective employees because personality attributes are so important in sales work. Since agents and brokers usually work without supervision, they must be able to plan their time well and have the initiative to locate new clients.

An insurance agent who shows sales ability and leadership may become a sales manager in a local office. A few advance to agency superintendent or executive positions. However, many who have built up a good clientele prefer to remain in sales work. Some, particularly in the property/casualty field, establish their own independent agencies or brokerage firms.

Salaries

The median annual earnings of salaried insurance sales workers is about $31,500, but workers can start as low as in the teens and range up to $77,000 a year or more.

Most independent agents are paid on a commission only basis. Sales workers who are employees of an agency may be paid in one of three ways—salary only, salary plus commission, or salary plus bonus. Commissions, however, are the most common form of compensation, especially for experienced agents. The amount of the commission depends on the type and amount of insurance sold and whether the transaction is a new policy or a renewal. Bonuses are usually awarded when agents meet their production goals or when an agency's profit goals are met.

Many agencies also pay for automobile and transportation expenses, conventions and meetings, promotion and marketing expenses, and retirement plans.

All agents are legally responsible for any mistakes they make, and independent agents must purchase their own insurance to cover damages from their errors and omissions.

Real Estate Sales

Buying or selling a home or an investment property is not only one of the most important financial events in peoples' lives but one of the most complex transactions as well. As a result, people generally seek the help of real estate agents or brokers.

Real estate agents and brokers need to have a thorough knowledge of the housing market in their communities. They must know which neighborhoods will best fit their clients' needs and budgets. They must be familiar with local zoning and tax laws and know how to obtain financing. Agents and brokers also act as intermediaries for negotiations between buyers and sellers.

Brokers are independent businesspeople who, for a fee, sell real estate owned by others. They also rent and manage properties. In closing sales, brokers often provide buyers with information on loans to finance their purchases. They also arrange for title searches and for meetings between buyers and sellers when details of the transactions are agreed upon and the new owners take possession. Having the knowledge, resourcefulness, and creativity in arranging financing that is most favorable to the prospective buyer often means the difference between success and failure in closing a sale.

In some cases, agents assume the responsibilities in closing sales, but, in many areas, this is done by lawyers, lenders, or title companies. Brokers also manage their own offices, supervise associate agents, advertise properties, and handle other business matters.

Real estate agents are generally independent sales workers who provide their services to a licensed broker on a contract basis. In return, the broker pays the agent a portion of the commission earned from property sold through the firm by the agent. Today, relatively few agents receive salaries as employees of brokers or realty firms. Instead, most agents derive their incomes solely from commissions.

Responsibilities in Real Estate Sales

When you work with customers in real estate, the most important thing is learning how to listen to their needs. Clients will have their dream homes in mind with wish lists that describe everything they want—but often it's not what they can afford. You have to go through that list and determine their priorities. Is it necessary for them to have four bedrooms, for example, or will three do? Do they want one story or two? Do they need a room to serve as an office?

At that point, the agent or broker calls in a mortgage broker, and they go through the buyers' qualifications and see where they sit financially. It's very important to prequalify buyers. You can then see whether they can afford a $100,000 house, for example, or something more or less costly.

The next step is to go to the computer and pull up everything that's in that price range. Determine the most viable possibilities in that price range and start from the top and work your way down. It's often a process of elimination.

Then, the house hunting begins. Agents spend a lot of time showing homes to prospective buyers. Once a home has been found and the contract has been signed by both parties, the real estate broker or agent must see to it that all special terms of the contract are met before the closing date. For example, if the seller has agreed to a home inspection or a termite and radon inspection, the agent must make sure that this is done. Also, if the seller has agreed to any repairs, the broker or agent must see to it that they have been made, otherwise the sale cannot be completed.

Increasingly, brokers and agents must handle environmental problems or make sure the properties they are selling meets environmental regulations. For example, while many other details are handled by loan officers, attorneys, or other people, the agent may be responsible for dealing with problems such as lead paint on the walls.

Because brokers and agents must have properties to sell, they spend a significant amount of time obtaining listings (owner agreements to place properties for sale with the firm). They spend time on the telephone exploring leads gathered from various sources, including personal contacts. When listing property for sale, agents and brokers make comparisons with similar properties that recently sold to determine fair market value.

Most real estate agents and brokers sell residential property. A few, usually those from large firms or specialized small firms, sell commercial, industrial, agricultural, or other types of real estate. Each specialty requires knowledge of that particular type of property and clientele.

Although real estate agents and brokers generally work in offices, much of their time is spent outside the office showing properties to customers, analyzing properties for sale, meeting with prospective clients, researching the state of the market, inspecting properties for appraisal, and performing a wide range of other duties. Brokers provide office space, but agents generally furnish their own automobiles.

Qualifications and Training

All states and the District of Columbia require real estate agents and brokers to be licensed. This means that every prospective agent must be a high school graduate, at least eighteen years old, and pass a written test. The examination, which is more comprehensive for brokers than for agents, includes questions on basic real estate transactions and on laws affecting the sale of property.

Most states require candidates for the general sales license to complete at least thirty hours of classroom instruction and those seeking the broker's license to complete ninety hours of formal training in addition to a specified amount of experience in selling real estate (generally one to three years). Some states waive the experience requirements for the broker's license for applicants who have bachelor's degrees in real estate. A small but increasing number of states require that agents have sixty hours of college credit—roughly the equivalent of an associate's degree. State licenses generally must be renewed every year or two, usually without reexamination. Many states, however, require continuing education for license renewal.

Personality traits are as important as formal credentials. Brokers look for applicants who possess a pleasant personality, honesty, and a neat appearance. Maturity, tact, and enthusiasm for the job are required in order to motivate prospective customers in this keenly competitive field. Agents should also be well organized and detail oriented, as well as have a good memory for names, faces, and business details such as taxes, zoning regulations, and local land-use laws.

The beginner usually learns the practical aspects of the job under the direction of an experienced agent. This includes focusing on the use of computers to locate or list available properties or identify sources of financing.

Many firms offer formal training programs for both beginners and experienced agents. Larger firms generally offer more extensive programs than smaller firms. More than a thousand universities, colleges, and junior colleges offer courses in real estate. At some, a student can earn an associate's or bachelor's degree with a major in real estate; several offer advanced degrees.

Many local real estate boards (that are members of the National Association of Realtors) sponsor courses covering the fundamentals and legal aspects of the field. Advanced courses in appraisal, mortgage financing, property development and management, and other subjects also are available through various affiliates of the National Association of Realtors.

Salaries

Commissions on sales are the main source of earnings for real estate agents and brokers. Few receive a salary. The commission varies according to the type of property and its value. The percentage paid for the sale of farm or commercial properties or unimproved land is usually higher than that for selling a home.

Commissions may be divided among several agents and brokers. The broker and the agent in the firm that obtained the listing generally share their parts of the commission when the property is sold; the broker and the agent in the firm that made the sale also generally share their parts of the commission.

Although an agent's share varies greatly from one firm to another, often it is about 50 or 60 percent of the total amount received by the firm. The agent who both lists and sells the property maximizes his or her commission.

Real estate agents and brokers who usually work full-time have median yearly earnings of about $31,500. But earnings could be as low as $10,000 or less or run up to $75,000 or more.

A beginner's earnings are often irregular because a few weeks or even months may go by without a sale. Although some brokers allow an agent a drawing account against future earnings, this practice is unusual with new employees. The beginner, therefore, should have enough money to live on for about six months or until commissions increase.

The Downsides

In addition to lean income periods, sometimes a deal can fall through at the last minute. For example, buyers might get pre-qualified for a mortgage, based on income and debt, if any, and other factors. But another financial examination is conducted just before closing. If the buyers have purchased new furniture, for example, or in some other way changed their financial pictures, it can kill the deal.

Agents also have to be very careful when dealing with new clients who are strangers. This is especially true for women realtors. Brokers will encourage their agents to work in pairs if possible and to always arrange the first meeting with the client to take place at the office, not at the property. Another precaution is to avoid taking anybody in your car. Instead, have the clients follow you in their own cars.

There are always times when you may show a client twenty properties without selling a thing, but don't look at this as wasted time. Rather, it gives you a chance to increase your knowledge of different properties new to the market. You can always use that information for the next call.

Travel Agents

Out of all the industries worldwide, travel and tourism continue to grow at an astounding rate. In fact, according to the Travel Works for America Council, the travel industry is the second largest employer in the United States (the first being health services). Nearly everyone tries to take at least one vacation every year and many people travel frequently on business. Some travel for education or for that special honeymoon or anniversary trip.

Constantly changing airfares and schedules, a proliferation of vacation packages, and business/pleasure trip combinations make travel planning frustrating and time consuming. Many travelers, therefore, turn to travel agents, who can make the best possible travel arrangements for them. Depending on the needs of the client, travel agents give advice on destinations; make arrangements for transportation, hotel accommodations, car rentals, tours, and recreation; or plan the right vacation package or a combination business and pleasure trip.

They may also provide information on weather conditions, restaurants, and tourist attractions and recreation. For international travel, agents also provide information on customs regulations, required papers (passports, visas, and certificates of vaccination), and currency exchange rates. Travel agents must learn about all the different destinations, modes of transportation, hotels, resorts, and cruises, then work to match their customers' needs with the services travel providers offer.

Travel agents generally work in an office and deal with customers in person or over the phone. First they listen to the needs of their customers, then try to develop the best package for each person. They may work with a variety of clients—affluent, sophisticated travelers, or first-timers such as students trying to save money and travel on a budget. They could book a simple, round-trip air ticket for a person traveling alone or handle arrangements for hundreds of people traveling to attend a convention or conference.

Some travel agents are generalists; they handle any or all situations. Others specialize in a particular area such as cruise ships or corporate travel. Travel agents gather information from different sources. They use computer databases, attend trade shows, and read trade magazines. They also visit resorts or locations to get firsthand knowledge about a destination.

Travel agents have to keep up with rapidly changing fares and rates, and they have to know who offers the best packages and service. Their most important concern is the satisfaction of their clients.

Since travel providers understand that travel agents are more likely to sell what they have enjoyed, most travel agents are offered free trips to help familiarize them with a particular cruise line, safari adventure, exclusive resort, or ecological tour. Travel agents also receive discounted travel on other business trips, as well as on their own vacations.

Travel agents often base recommendations on their own travel experiences or those of colleagues or clients. Travel agents may visit hotels, resorts, and restaurants to judge, firsthand, their comfort, cleanliness, and quality of food and service.

The Downsides

The downside, however, according to many travel agents, is that they seldom have enough free time to do all the traveling they would like to do. They are often tied to their desks, especially during peak travel periods such as the summer or important holidays. A newcomer would get to take at least one week a year, more once they've gained some seniority.

The work can also be frustrating at times. Customers might not always know what they want, or their plans can change, and as a result, the travel agent might have to cancel or reroute destinations that had already been set. There are times when things go wrong. There could be a snow-in at an airport and people miss their connections or someone in the family becomes ill and they have to cancel the whole cruise reservation at the last minute.

In addition, changes in airline policies for paying travel agents a percentage of flight ticket prices have severely affected income levels. The Internet has also affected business for travel agents because more and more people are making their own reservations on-line.

Qualifications and Training

Formal or specialized training is becoming increasingly important for travel agents since few agencies are willing to train people on the job. Many vocational schools offer three- to twelve- week full-time programs, as well as evening and Saturday programs. Travel courses are also offered in public adult education programs and in community and four-year colleges. A few colleges offer bachelor's and master's degrees in travel and tourism.

Although few college courses relate directly to the travel industry, a college education is sometimes desired by employers. Courses in computer science, geography, foreign languages, and history are most useful. Courses in accounting and business management are also important, especially for those who expect to manage or start their own travel agencies. Several home-study courses provide a basic understanding of the travel industry.

The American Society of Travel Agents (ASTA) and the Institute of Certified Travel Agents (ICTA) offer a travel correspondence course. Travel agencies also provide on-the-job training for their employees. A significant part of this focuses on computer instruction. These computer skills are required by employers to operate airline reservation systems.

Experienced travel agents can take an advanced course (leading to the designation of Certified Travel Counselor) offered by the Institute of Certified Travel Agents. The institute awards a certificate to those completing an eighteen-month, part-time course. It also offers certification, called Designation of Competence, in North American, Western European, Caribbean, or South Pacific tours.

Travel experience is an asset since personal knowledge about a city or foreign country often helps to influence clients' travel plans. Experience as an airline reservation agent is also a good background for a travel agent. Travel agents need good selling skills. Additionally, they must be pleasant and patient and able to gain the confidence of clients.

Beginners often start working side by side with someone more experienced in the agency. They might be placed in a specific department handling, for example, European travel, cruises, car rental, or airfares. Much of their time will be spent coordinating and arranging details.

Travel agents must also compete with all the other agents in the field and need to know how to promote their services. This may be accomplished by presenting slides or movies to social and special interest groups, arranging advertising displays, and suggesting company-sponsored trips to business managers.

Those who start their own agencies generally have experience in an established agency. They must generally gain formal supplier or corporation approval before they can receive commissions. Suppliers or corporations are organizations of airlines, ship lines, or rail lines. The Airlines Reporting Corporation, for example, is the approving body for airlines. To gain approval, an agency must be in operation, be financially sound, and employ at least one experienced manager/travel agent.

Salaries

Salaries vary according to the region in which you work and your experience. Depending on the agency, you could start out on an hourly wage or a yearly salary. Some travel agents prefer to work on a commission basis. That way, the more trips they sell, the more money they earn. A salary plus commission provides the best compensation combination.

Travel agents who are good salespeople can also earn bonuses or more free or discounted trips. If your pay is initially low, it can be offset by this added benefit.

Experience, sales ability, and the size and location of the agency determine the salary of a travel agent. According to a Louis Harris survey, conducted for *Travel Weekly* magazine, annual earnings for travel agents are as follows:

less than one year experience—$16,400

from one to three years—$20,400

from three to five years—$22,300

from five to ten years—$26,300

more than ten years—$32,600

Salaried agents usually have standard benefits, such as insurance coverage and paid vacations. Self-employed agents must provide these for themselves.

Earnings of travel agents who own their agencies depend mainly on commissions from airlines and other carriers, cruise lines, tour operators, and hotels. Commissions for domestic travel arrangements, cruises, hotels, sight-seeing tours, and car rentals are about 10 percent of the total sale; for international travel, they're about 11 percent. They may also charge clients a service fee for the time and expense involved in planning a trip.

Words from the Pros

Meet Marty Gorelick, Computer Hardware Sales Professional

Marty Gorelick has a bachelor of arts degree from Long Island University in Brooklyn, New York, and eight years' experience in computer hardware sales. He has also attended seminars from all of the major computer manufacturers: Compaq, IBM, Hewlett Packard, Sony, Apple, and NEC. He is account manager for county government sales at GE Capital IT Solutions in Miami, Florida, where he services Metro-Dade, Broward, and Pasco Counties, plus all cities, towns, and villages within these areas.

"The computer industry is constantly changing," he says. "It is the fastest-growing industry in the world. Every person on our planet is connected in one way or another. Computers have made communications possible at lightning speed.

"Scientists, doctors, engineers, lawyers, manufacturers, teachers, those in the arts and every other element of society operate at higher levels of proficiency than ever before because of computers. For example, a doctor in Seattle can supervise a surgical procedure in an operating room located in Atlanta through the aid of a computer hook up. Ten short years ago, this was impossible. Using a process called computer-aided design (CAD), engineers can design structures that will withstand stress far beyond their intended safety limits. Police can track known law offenders well outside of their jurisdictions and notify other law enforcement officers of potential problems. This, by far, is only the tip of the iceberg. Computer applications are endless.

"A typical day for me begins when I arrive at my office about 6:30 A.M. After running the branch's allocation reports for all the salespeople in our office, I check my voice mail for any emergency issues that must be addressed quickly. An example might be a critical shipment that hasn't arrived on time or a file server that has developed a problem and is inoperable. These situations demand my immediate attention. If both these situations exist, I'll contact our Atlanta facility to run a tracer and our service department to check out the server on the first call of the day.

"I read my E-mail messages next. It's not unusual to have between five and fifteen messages ranging from company updates to manufacturer price changes to additions and deletions from any number of vendors. Since I give my E-mail address to my customers, I might see a request for a quotation on a product or clarification of a service agreement or a question about the configuration of a Mini-Tower Computer with 32MB memory, 2.5GB hard drive, and an 8X CD-ROM. Some messages require a response as soon as possible; others can be addressed during the course of my regular business day.

"Next stop is my in box, which usually contains a collection of faxes that have arrived since I left the office yesterday. These faxes could contain purchase orders, manufacturer promotional notices, seminar information, or news of a prospective customer looking for a great reseller like ours! All this, and the clock has not yet struck 8 A.M.

"Now, the doors swing open, and my fellow employees arrive. The phones go off night ring, and our customers start calling in. We field calls concerning products, service, availability, additions, deletions, and changes in orders.

"During the course of the day, the staff may all meet for a quick meeting to discuss a change in plans concerning a new company procedure. Our regularly scheduled sales meeting takes place at 8:30 A.M. sharp each Wednesday. This is when we discuss our progress as a group and host a manufacturer who is introducing a new product or products.

"We constantly update our price list to remain the most competitive reseller in the marketplace. I do a special electronic price list every sixty days. This process usually takes me anywhere from three to four working days. I also provide a manuscript of five thousand plus items from a third-party vendor. On any given day, I may accompany a manufacturer downtown to the county building where we will call on a number of departments that have requested information or a demonstration of a new item.

"Afternoons are generally reserved for cleaning up all unfinished projects, faxing quotes, looking for odd items that appear on purchase orders, and filing away purchase orders and invoices. My day ends about the time that local traffic starts to build on the highway. This represents a ten-plus-hour day, five days a week, four point three weeks a month. To say this is a hectic day is putting it mildly. However, if you enjoy what you do, it can be and *is* a labor of love.

"The most enjoyable part of my position is helping my customers understand their needs in respect to the use of the equipment. An example would be a customer who is interested in a laptop computer in order to do presentations at remote sites versus a client needing a laptop for communicating with his home base. One would need a CD-ROM; the other might only need a fax/modem. Some may need both.

"If I had to pick a project I least like to perform, it's the amount of paperwork that is a necessary evil in the day-to-day flow of business. The upside of my business is the satisfaction of being productive while helping others do the same. When I complete a project with confidence and in a timely manner so my customers can enjoy productivity, I take a moment to sit back and breathe easy.

"The downside is always the fact of being in a race with the clock. I try to never let the clock win. I also refuse to let a discontinued product stop me from saying to customers that I can't fill their needs. Somewhere out there is a replacement part. All salespeople are part detective. We look until we find what we need to help our customers.

"For those who are considering entering my world, I would say to be prepared to plan for a very exciting career. Technology advances as fast as you can absorb yesterday's breakthroughs. Pick a school that offers the career path that you wish to follow (sales and marketing, computer network engineering, or service and repair). Attend as many seminars in the field as possible. Read as many journals that pertain to your area of interest. Spend as much time as you can afford, talking to those around you in that particular field. Don't be afraid to roll up your sleeves and get your hands dirty. Ask a million questions. Experiment with the knowledge you've gained. Share your findings with others, and never stop learning."

Meet Donna Maas, President, CEO, and Sales Professional

Donna Maas's formal studies include interior architecture, design, drafting, and oil painting. With a background in graphic art, she designs all marketing materials and packaging for MAAS Polishing Systemes™ of Willowbrook, Illinois. She serves as president and CEO of the company. After six years of using various cleaning and polishing products and always wishing for something better, Maas asked a chemist to assist her in formulating a product that worked. The end result is MAAS Polishing Creme, a product that quickly restores all metals, fiberglass, Plexiglas, and dull oxidized paint work to an unusually brilliant finish. "Little did I realize how this innovative formula would revolutionize the polishing products industry," she says.

"The job is glamorous, hectic, and unpredictable," Maas explains. "My role encompasses product development, designing marketing materials, and fielding calls from major retailers while maintaining balance in the offices, warehouse, and factory. This, combined with extensive traveling and television appearances on QVC to demonstrate my products, requires tremendous stamina. Everyone within the company, from my executive assistant to the shipping department, will tell you that every project I tackle must be treated with urgency, requiring immediate attention. This keeps my office personnel (and myself) operating at an unusually fast pace.

"By the third year in business, I experienced an 800 percent growth on my initial investment," she says. "It is tremendously fulfilling to obtain such rapid success and worldwide recognition. I would have to think long and hard if asked what the downside of my career is because I can't think of anything!

"I would advise others who wish to get into this field to stay focused! The most difficult thing for an entrepreneur to do is to focus. You have so many things coming at you all at once. I have learned to concentrate on the most promising opportunities. When you become scattered and attempt to address every opportunity, your success is hindered."

Meet Jim LeClair, Business Owner and Sales Manager

Jim LeClair is the owner and sales manager for Advanced Computer Services in Lawrence, Kansas. He earned a high school diploma and took some secondary accounting and business classes. He has also engaged in ongoing seminars and classes, which are offered by suppliers to enhance sales, technical training, and product knowledge.

"I was burned out on retail and on working for others," he says, "so my wife and I decided to form our own business. She had a strong computer background, and I had more of the business background. We felt our strengths would complement one another. Our company consists of training and network installations and network design to integration, support, and fiber optics (to name a few).

"We have five employees. Our store hours are Monday through Friday, from 8 A.M. until 5 P.M. The atmosphere is as relaxed as possible—business casual Monday through Thursday, casual on Friday. Our busiest time of the year is summer.

"I try to keep politics out of the workplace and am flexible with my employees and their families as much as possible. Overtime, for instance, is kept to a minimum.

"A day can change within the first five minutes you walk in the door. You have to be able to juggle things around to grease the squeakiest wheel. I generally arrive at 7 A.M. and leave between 6:30 and 7 P.M., spending approximately 30 percent of my time administering to the customers' needs, 40 percent working on sales, and 30 percent on the day-to-day activities of running the business.

"What I like best is seeing how happy the customer is when we say this is how the network will work, and then the network performs as well or better than we anticipated. What I like least is having to discipline employees or contemplate lost sales.

"To be successful in this kind of work, it's very important to keep abreast of the current technology at all times, to be a good listener, to be flexible, to be able to read people, and to understand what they really want, not what they say they want. You have to be able to think quickly on your feet and have a semiaggressive nature. You just can't take no for an answer. Still, you must sell the customers what they want. Don't try to sell people something that isn't right for them, just because you can make some money.

"I'd advise those who are considering computer sales to be honest, to be fair, and to *always* do a good job. Our business has grown because we have gained the trust of both our customers and our employees."

Meet Kathryn M. McKenzie, Sales Representative

Kathryn McKenzie received her bachelor of arts degree in history from Davidson College in Davidson, North Carolina. She has recently begun working toward her master's degree in museum studies/textile conservation at the Fashion Institute of Technology. Presently, she is employed as a sales representative for Victor Innovatex/Studio 180, a mill that makes fabric specifically for the office furniture market.

"I was working for an office furniture dealer as marketing manager and decided that I wanted to pursue a career in textiles," she says. "I was called by a headhunter, who asked if I would be interested in a sales position for a textile mill. The company is based in Quebec, Canada, and I would work from home as a sales rep for the Northeast. My immediate response was 'No way' because I didn't want a sales position and I didn't have the space to work at home. Then I reconsidered and decided that I should at least go to the interview. Much to my surprise I got the position and have been enjoying it ever since!

"I saw the position as a challenge and a chance to improve my business skills. I never really enjoyed talking with strangers and was forced to do that on the very first day. I wanted to develop strategic thinking skills and have certainly had the chance to do that as well. It was important that I work for a company that actually produced something. Becoming involved in the textile industry was particularly attractive to me because I have always loved fabric.

"Previously, I had worked for an office furniture dealer for six years and had been given the opportunity to take on a variety of jobs. I started working there as a project assistant as part of a project management team. The project was for Morgan Bank, which was just finishing the construction of its new office headquarters, a fifty-story building. Eventually I handled the acquisition of furnishings and the move for the last five floors. Then I went into the marketing end of things, working on proposals and contracts. Finally, I took on the role of marketing manager and handled proposals, contracts, marketing literature, events, and so forth. All of these job experiences enhanced my skills, while the exposure to the ace sales force at the dealership served me well. Also, since I stayed within the same industry, I was able to use my knowledge of the market to my advantage.

"As with most jobs, my job is a mix of stress and pleasure. The stress is in meeting numbers and objectives set by me and the sales manager; the pleasure is in being involved in the design process and showing exciting products and capabilities to my customers.

"There are no typical days! Generally every day starts out with a battery of phone calls, then meetings with customers or internal meetings with design staff. After each customer meeting, I write a report and send it to the sales manager and design group so that we are all clear about what customers have seen, what they want, and what their expectations are.

"As the sales representative, I am the liaison, the communicator, the project manager, and the problem solver. For the most part, my days are fairly relaxed, unless there is a problem to resolve. My work week averages forty hours, but some days are extra long, especially when traveling great distances to meet with certain customers.

"When seeing customers, the work atmosphere is exciting. It's definitely enjoyable taking customers out for those necessary business lunches! However, it's tedious when you've traveled a distance and no one bothers to show up.

"What I like most about my work is that I'm involved in textiles and that the clients I deal with are especially nice. I love the challenge of discovering just how my company can fulfill a need for a customer. I enjoy the fact that the days and hours are somewhat flexible, that I set my own schedule. I feel comfortable knowing that the results (sales) are based on my efforts and the efforts of the design team. I like building relationships with customers and meeting new people.

"Initially I enjoyed the travel, but as time has gone on, it has become less exciting. I think it has more to do with the familiarity of those places and sometimes the hassles involved in getting to some of the far-flung places you have to go.

"My advice to others pursuing a career in sales is to take on the challenges but to think about the work environment or corporate culture you are entering. Sometimes you never know until you get there, but usually there are inklings of what a place will be like. Think about whether you really can work at home and whether you want your boss down the hall or in another country. I never realized what an impact these conditions would have on me.

"But whatever the circumstances, I would say 'Go for it'—you only live once, and life is not a race. It doesn't matter how you get to the finish line, just so long as you feel you have lived your life completely. If it doesn't work out, chalk it up to experience. If it does work out, then you are all the better for it."

Meet Don Godshaw, Owner/President and Sales Professional

Don Godshaw attended Lakeland College in Plymouth, Wisconsin. He majored in business administration and economics. After spending nineteen years in sales, marketing, and product development for the textiles, bag, and sporting goods industries, he now serves as owner and president of his own company, Travelon, based in Des Plaines, Illinois.

"I was assigned the duties of president of Travelon when the existing president was dismissed," says Godshaw. "Then after running the business for several months, the board chairman, in a surprise move, actually promoted me to president. Since that time, I have purchased the company, and now, in addition to president, I am owner and chairperson.

"Several things have contributed to my career path in sporting goods, sales, textiles, and bag manufacturing," he says. "Early childhood involvement in the sporting goods retail business, a love for skiing, and a talent for sales are three of them.

"In my early days in the sporting goods industry, I worked in a ski shop and dealt with all aspects of that sport. After my employer discovered my talent for sales, he no longer allowed me to spend significant time working in the stock room or service departments. The majority of my days were then spent in sales, display, merchandising, and purchasing. During those first few years, my involvement with backpacks, tents, sleeping bags, and other outdoor equipment fostered my passion for the luggage and travel wear industry. I was always keenly interested in innovative approaches in the backpacking or luggage industries—constantly looking for better and more organized ways of featuring merchandise.

"My early backpacking days in northern Canada included a great deal of experience carrying a canvas pack with leather shoulder straps and a tumpline. (A tumpline is a functional but rather primitive device that transfers the weight of a backpack to the front of your head and you carry substantial weight using your neck muscles.) Unfortunately, when you carry a backpack with a tumpline you are constantly looking at the ground in front of you and not the spectacular scenery. This convinced me that there had to be a better way, although at that time I never considered that recognizing that problem would become part of my career path.

"Many people on the outside think this business is very glamorous. I invite them to spend several days in my shoes. Overseas travel to distant exotic places includes putting up with bad water, uncomfortable hotel rooms, and weeks away from family and friends. I spend approximately 35 percent of my year on international business travel. A typical workday in Asia starts at 6:30 A.M. with a quick meal and then off to the factory, where I will spend the entire day supervising new product design, negotiating pricing, and solving quality problems. There is a tremendous amount of communication with our clients and our office. After ten to fourteen hours at a factory, I will typically return to my hotel, contact my office, and go to sleep. It is not an easy business but one that offers substantial opportunities for creative, hard-working firms.

"While in my office in Des Plaines, Illinois, a typical day begins with my reading ten to twenty pages of overseas E-mail or faxes at 7 A.M. If our vice president of sales is in town, I will typically meet with her and get updated on all of the sales activity that relates to Travelon branded products. If there are specific questions regarding any topic ranging from sales, credit, new product designs, or office politics, I'll get involved as needed. As the day progresses, my office door is open, and the flow of people with questions or comments is endless. Our product managers are given specific guidelines as to how to handle most aspects of the business, but many situations require deviation from standard operating procedure, so I stay closely involved with most aspects of our business. The pace is hectic but exceptionally satisfying, in good part because I have been lucky enough to surround myself with a team of dynamic executives (mostly female) who are intelligent, trustworthy, and passionate about our business.

"The atmosphere in which I work is tremendously important to me. We have a business casual dress policy in our office and try to take that casual attitude into our entire organization. Although we have twenty-five employees and need to have some established rules, we basically hire people who are diligent self-starters who do not require constant direction. There are rarely any closed-door meetings, and communications between all levels of the company are very clear. Our people realize that working together positively accomplishes much more than talking about who is doing what to whom. The staff works together like a championship-level sports team. The camaraderie and support is like nothing I've seen in my prior business experiences. I'm tremendously proud of the way our people work selflessly towards a common goal.

"The aspect of my work that I like best is the creative merchandising and marketing side—determining a target customer, developing a product strategy, and then presenting that concept with the strength of our organization behind it. It's tremendously satisfying to know that all departments—product design, manufacturing, importation, product management, distribution, and finance—are 100 percent ready, willing, and able to work together to successfully complete every project.

"My least favorite aspect of our business is dealing with those customers who appear to feel that they are doing us a favor in allowing us to sell to them. I look to our relationships with our customers as strategic partnerships, and a partnership needs to be good for both parties. Once in a while, we deal with clients who feel that only their needs must be satisfied and that our needs are secondary.

"I attribute our success to the highly talented people we've been fortunate enough to be able to assemble. It's relatively simple to build some good products in any field but extremely difficult over the long-term to hold together a good organization of people. As a leader, I realize it is my job to try to be considerate of the financial and emotional needs of our staff members. With that accomplished, we can continue to have a winning team."

For More Information

By contacting the following list of professional associations, you can obtain more information about each category of sales.

Retail Sales

Information on careers in retail sales may be obtained from the personnel offices of local stores, from state merchants' associations, or from local unions of the United Food and Commercial Workers International Union. In addition, general information about retailing is available from:

National Retail Federation
701 Pennsylvania Avenue NW
Washington, DC 20004

Services Sales

For details about employment opportunities for services sales representatives, contact employers who sell services in your area.

For information on careers and scholarships in hotel management and sales, contact:

The American Hotel and Motel Association (AH&MA)
Information Center
1201 New York Avenue NW
Washington, DC 20005

Manufacturing and Wholesale

Information on manufacturers' agents is available from:

Sales and Marketing Management International
Statler Office Tower
Cleveland, OH 44115

Insurance Sales

General occupational information about insurance agents and brokers is available from the home office of many life and casualty insurance companies. Information on state licensing requirements may be obtained from the department of insurance at any state capitol.

Information about careers in life insurance is available from:

National Association of Life Underwriters
1922 F Street NW
Washington, DC 20006

For information about insurance sales careers in independent agencies and brokerages, contact:

National Association of Professional Insurance Agents
400 North Washington Street
Alexandria, VA 22314

For information about certification programs, contact:

American Society of Chartered Life Underwriters and
    Chartered Financial Consultants
270 Bryn Mawr Avenue
Bryn Mawr, PA 19010

Society of Certified Insurance Counselors
3630 North Hills Drive
Austin, TX 78731

Society of Chartered Property and Casualty Underwriters
Kahler Hall
720 Providence Road
P.O. Box 3009
Malvern, PA 19355

Real Estate Sales

Details on licensing requirements for real estate agents, brokers, and appraisers are available from most local real estate and appraiser organizations or from the state real estate commission or board.

For more information about opportunities in real estate work, contact:

National Association of Realtors
777 Fourteenth Street NW
Washington, DC 20005

Information on careers, licensing, and certification requirements in real estate appraising is available from:

American Society of Appraisers
P.O. Box 17265
Washington, DC 20041

Appraisal Institute
875 North Michigan Avenue, Suite 2400
Chicago, IL 60611

Travel Agents

For information on careers in the travel industry, write to:

American Society of Travel Agents
1101 King Street
Alexandria, VA 22314

Association of Retail Travel Agents
1745 Jefferson Davis Highway, Suite 300
Arlington, VA 22202

Institute of Certified Travel Agents
148 Linden Street
P.O. Box 56
Wellesley, MA 02181

CHAPTER TWO

Careers in Public Relations and Fund-Raising

The most amazing feature of American life is its boundless publicity. Everybody has to meet everybody, and they seem to enjoy this enormity. CARL JUNG

HELP WANTED: PUBLIC RELATIONS COORDINATOR
Chicago-based firm seeks professional with three years of experience in communications, media relations, or public relations positions. Strong business-to-business technology or information systems background preferred. We seek someone who is adept at strategic thinking, plan development, and implementation.

Excellent feature and article writing skills with strong knowledge of print communications (newsletter, press releases, magazines, journals), direct mail, image building, conference marketing, and advertising and promotional copywriting are required. Creativity and a fresh approach are essential as are desktop publishing and previous production experience. We offer competitive wages and a strong benefits package. Forward your resume with salary history to us immediately.

Public Relations

You might be surprised to learn that the concept of public relations is hardly a new invention. It goes all the way back to 1787, during the time of the Constitutional Convention. And in the 1800s, both the North and the South made use of the media during the Civil War in an attempt to persuade the populace to adopt their way of thinking.

Today, the goal of public relations remains the same—to sway the public in a particular direction, or to build, maintain, and promote positive relationships between two factions: the agencies (or companies) and the public.

Public Relations Professionals

Public relations professionals may operate as self-employed consultants or as employees of public relations companies. They may also find work in the PR departments of a variety of entities, such as political parties, nonprofit organizations, hospitals, colleges and universities, trade unions, financial institutions, social service organizations, or clothing companies.

Business and industry rely on corporate public relations to educate the public about their products and services. And since nonprofit organizations do not generally advertise, they count on public service announcements provided by public relations professionals to get their "word out."

Job Settings

The work of a public relations practitioner falls into six primary categories:

1. *Research*. This includes all of the preliminary work that is undertaken to determine what the client's goals are and to

map out a plan to achieve them. Library research, client interviews, surveys, opinion polls, and collecting data are all part of this.

2. *Program work.* Once the research is completed, a plan is set up.

3. *Writing and editing.* This may come in the form of press releases, presentations to clients, internal memos, reports, or magazine articles.

4. *Special events.* Included in this category are press conferences, special appearances, and autograph signings. All are carefully orchestrated to gain the greatest amount of attention.

5. *Media placement.* It is important to select the most important information to release, choose a good time to release it, and send it to the most advantageous receiver.

6. *Fund-raising.* Fund-raising is what sustains nonprofit organizations. Possible events include membership drives, direct solicitation, and benefit banquets.

Those who work as generalists in the field must be able to perform a wide array of duties, all at the same time. On any given week they may write press releases for one client, design a brochure for another, approach an editor for a third, meet with a talk show host for a fourth, implement a promotion for a fifth, set up a press conference for a sixth, put together a press kit for a seventh, work out the beginnings of a client contact for an eighth, and field media questions for a ninth!

In the governmental arena, public relations specialists may be called press secretaries, communications specialists, or information officers. A senator's press secretary informs the elected official's constituents of his or her accomplishments and responds to questions from the media and the press. The press secretary schedules and appears at press conferences and issues statements from his or her superior.

Qualifications and Training

Although there is no defined training program for public relations specialists, it is wise to combine a bachelor's degree with some public relations experience, particularly internships. Professionals in this field may have college majors in journalism, advertising, public relations, or communications. Some companies may express a preference for someone with a master's degree in business administration.

Typical courses include public relations principles and techniques; public relations management and administration, including organizational development; writing, emphasizing news releases, proposals, annual reports, scripts, speeches, and related items; visual communications, including desktop publishing and computer graphics; and research, emphasizing social science research and survey design and implementation.

Salaries

Median yearly earnings for full-time public relations specialists average about $32,000. A recent College Placement Council salary survey found that new college graduates entering the public relations field were offered average beginning salaries of $21,000.

According to a recent salary survey by the Public Relations Journal, public relations managers averaged $44,000.

In the federal government, individuals with bachelor's degrees start at about $23,000; those with master's degrees begin at $28,000. Those in managerial positions average about $46,000. A press secretary's salary will generally fall between $20,000 and $70,000.

Words from the Pros

Meet Tracy Larrua, Senior Account Executive

Tracy Larrua is a senior account executive for Macy & Associates, a public relations firm based in Venice, California. Larrua attended a performing arts high school, then entered business college but ended up working at an advertising agency instead of getting her degree. She quickly worked her way up the ladder in advertising after spending six years with a company called Ogilvie and Mather. She then began doing public relations work, which she has continued for the past twelve years.

"My typical day is spent writing pitch letters, developing story ideas for editors, and adding/deleting/updating our media database to be as up-to-date as possible as to what is going on with our clients," says Larrua. "While wearing a headset, I also make a lot of phone calls. The atmosphere is never relaxed. Actually, it is usually very high stress, but it's a fun stress. Our typical work week is forty-plus hours, but depending on client demand, work load, and editorial deadlines, it can easily turn into a sixty-plus week.

"Our company has the coolest environment," she says happily. "We operate from an old two-story brick firehouse that contains no offices but separate working areas. My space is a room with a view and two big windows that let in fresh air. The space is definitely very interactive. We have no doors. There are high ceilings and a very artsy conference room and lots of natural light. Whenever clients or friends come by, they tell us our offices look like a high-tech office space. We also play music throughout the day, and it's probably the most enjoyable and productive office environment I've ever had the pleasure of working in.

"The people I work with are great. Each of us brings different strengths to the group, and our personalities complement one

another. That's key when you work in a smaller office environment. The only downside for me is that our company specializes
in public relations for real estate and architectural clients. I enjoy
this, but I'd like to bring in more consumer-type clients in the
future, such as restaurants, hotels, and travel accounts.

"I would recommend that others who are interested in entering this profession get in on the ground floor and act like a
sponge. Soak up everything you can. As you start developing
your skills, you'll find yourself ascending. Also, stay flexible. This
industry has gone through all sorts of changes. Learn, adapt, and
adopt a fearless attitude."

Larrua also adds a word of caution: "If you aren't the 'people
type,' don't even consider getting into this business. You have to
be comfortable and persuasive in talking to people—all kinds of
people. Remember—your personality skills count for a lot in this
industry."

Meet Betsy Nichol, Owner of Nichol & Company

Betsy Nichol heads her own public relations agency, Nichol
& Company of New York. She earned her bachelor of science
degree in journalism from Boston University and has continued
to enhance her credentials through seminars and professional
workshops.

"I started my career as a journalist, as many public relations
experts do," Nichol says. "I was lucky enough to serve a three-
month internship at Fairchild Publications and then a full-time
position with one of its (then) daily newspapers, *Home Furnishings Daily* (now *HFN*). After three and a half years there, I was
recruited by a small public relations firm. Early on in my career,
someone told me I should have my own business, and at the time
I thought he was crazy, but as the years went by I realized that I
am one of those people who is better at being my own boss than
working for someone else.

"I was attracted to the field because of the fast pace and the realization that no two days would be alike. I knew I would always be learning about different subjects and meeting interesting people from all types of professions.

"I also like to communicate in writing, and good writing skills are essential in the PR business. There's never a dull moment in this business, and being successful requires many of the same skills as being a journalist. It's been an exciting journey.

"Being head of a public relations firm is very hectic," Nichol stresses. "The phone is always ringing, and you never know if it's a client with a crisis, an editor on a deadline, or an employee with a question. I'm continually monitoring my E-mail, talking on the phone, giving instructions to staff members, and receiving countless faxes, notes, and mailed items that require a quick response.

"I also spend a lot of time in meetings with clients or counseling them by phone or meeting with employees to guide their progress in achieving client objectives. Other time is spent on new business activities, keeping up with industry trends, and making internal changes accordingly. Much of my time is also spent on the endless administrative tasks involved in running a business. There is never enough time in a day.

"Networking is very important for my success. I attend and speak at many meetings, workshops, breakfasts, and lunches that can produce new business, provide insight into industry trends, and form strategic alliances that enable me to serve my clients better.

"The public relations business offers endless ways to express one's creativity. It also demands that one think strategically to help clients solve their problems. This keeps me on my toes and makes every day action packed.

"In running a business of twelve people, there is also a great sense of teamwork and caring among the staff members—not a typical office environment. The interaction produces exciting results and great fun.

"The downside is that we often have to cancel evening plans and work late to meet breaking deadlines.

"My advice to others who are considering this field is to work hard, be flexible, and be both patient and impatient in your quest for success."

Meet Karen Bierman, Publicist

Karen Bierman received a bachelor of arts degree from Cornell University in Ithaca, New York. She now works as a publicist at Planned Television Arts in New York.

"It was kind of a fluke that allowed me to begin working in the industry right after college," she says. "A friend of the family had interned at Columbia/TriStar and highly recommended it to me. I had always been a movie buff and liked the idea of PR, so I applied and got accepted. Luckily for me, it was at a time when there were very few interns, so I was really able to learn a lot and do a lot. The people that I worked with were great and always willing to talk to me about the industry.

"After my internship was over I went to Universal Films to learn more. Since the PR departments of film companies in New York are relatively small, it is difficult to get a full-time job. I decided to try working in the theater, as there were no jobs in film at the time. Through a contact I had made, I got a job with Actors Equity doing research. While I loved the company and they were wonderful teachers, I really wanted to stay in PR. I applied once again to all of the film companies and publicity agencies in New York and was offered a position at Baker Winokur Ryder PR (BWR). During my two and one half years there, I served as an office assistant, assistant publicist to the vice president of publicity/director of the New York office, and junior publicist.

"Public relations positions consist mainly of getting to know the client or the project you've been assigned to, as well as the media you'll be working with. This undoubtedly translates into making hundreds of phone calls each day scheduling photo shoots, screenings, interviews and personal appearances; securing invitations to events; getting clothing for the client to wear; and arranging travel and transportation. Depending on the project, there may be a lot of writing involved. Often, there are large numbers of faxes and mailings of press materials. Also, many publicists write their clients' bios and 'pitch' letters. In addition, publicists may be called upon to chaperone clients. This means taking them to all of their interviews and appearances and making sure that everything goes smoothly.

"The atmosphere can range from rather stressful to relaxed, depending on the project you are working on. When deadlines are approaching or you are working on a high-profile account, things are more demanding, but during the summer television hiatus, things can be quieter. Still, overall, the job involves long hours and many nights and weekends at work because the events that your clients attend are held after normal work hours and often times press junkets are held over the weekend. Frequently, you are required to bring your client to an early morning television interview and then go out late in the evening to a film premiere or store opening.

"I would stress to others that patience is truly a virtue in this business. It can be really difficult to get your foot in the door, so try to get internships over the summer and during the school year. Most schools will give you credit for these internships. And networking is also very important. If you meet people through internships or at parties, keep in touch with them. You never know who might be the one to help provide your big break. Also, many companies like to promote from within, so if you are offered a job that you think is beneath you, it might still be worthwhile to take it and prove to them that you are worthy of a promotion. It really helps to be an outgoing, vivacious person, as you really need to not only 'sell' your client but yourself as well. Remember that appearance is also important—you always want to dress as if you've already received that next promotion!"

Meet Joanne Levine, Public Relations Professional and Business Owner

"My company, Chicago area–based Lekas & Levine Public Relations, specializes in pursuing media publicity for small and mid-sized businesses. Media public relations is probably the most popular among clients but also the most stressful for the practitioner. Although I also write copy for brochures and business letters and plan some special events, 80 percent of my time is spent trying to help my clients make the news—that is, helping them to appear in newspapers, magazines, and trade publications, and on radio and television.

"My clients recognize that media publicity is a valuable tool to increase visibility of their products or services, while enhancing their images in the eyes of potential customers, suppliers, business associates, and peers. While paid advertising 'looks like an ad,' editorial appearances add credibility and help to establish the client as an authority in his or her respective field. Whether a fledgling entrepreneur or an established pillar of the business community, there are few people who wouldn't relish the opportunity to make a favorable impression in the news.

"On the other hand, my specialty is probably the least favorite among public relations practitioners. With an ad, you know what day it will appear, what size it will be, and exactly what it will say. With an article, I hold my breath until the client and I read it in the publication. With a taped interview on radio or television, I wait to see if anything was cut or taken out of context. While my press release and phone conversation with an editor might have been chock-full of the kind of information I hope they will relay to the public, there are no guarantees that this will be the case. I work with editors and writers who are always on deadline, always overworked, but nevertheless always looking for a good angle. For these reasons, my job can be stressful and sometimes plagued with problems that are completely out of my control.

"But when all goes well, there's nothing like it. I have seen the positive results of good, steady media campaigns time and time again. And more than once in a while, a really big media appearance can make an overnight difference in someone's business. The client is on cloud nine, his or her phones begin to ring off the hook with new business, and I am showered with praise and gratitude. I often get to know my clients well and enjoy friendly, upbeat working relationships with them. The knowledge that I am helping to make a client's business grow is very rewarding.

"Although a degree in journalism or communications is certainly desirable, in my particular case, I entered this career without any real planning. Even though I majored in English in college, I didn't really have any ambition to focus on public relations. When my children were babies, I didn't even work outside the home but joined various local community groups, such as Friends of the Parks, the PTA, and a Human Relations group. In the course of setting up a fund-raiser for one of the organizations, I was paired with a real life PR pro on the publicity committee. She really gave me an education, and I became fascinated with her skills. At the same time, my very creative brother was writing music, forming bands, and starting wacky side businesses. One of his companies created and marketed original adult board games that he designed. To test my new skills, each time he introduced a game, I sent out press releases to the media. The first game, Danger Island, even included me as one of the characters. When the reporters arrived, I became part of the story. We got spectacular local and national coverage.

"That first project really whet my appetite. From there, I began publicizing my husband's retail stores, more civic groups, and the like. One day, I thought about the fact that I was doing a great job and not getting paid for it. I recruited my brother's wife to help me, and we wrote a press release about two sisters-in-law who started a public relations company devoted to small businesses. We got an immediate response from the local chain of newspapers. They wrote a feature article about our company, even though we had no clients. The rest, they say, is history. From that initial article, the phone began to ring, and within a month or two, we had five clients. Its been word of mouth ever since.

"My sister-in-law stayed aboard for nine years and finally decided to return to her first love—teaching. She always felt that even if she did a great job pitching an idea to an editor, it was always the editor who determined how well we did our job. We were always caught in the middle—if the article was great, the client thought we were, too. If the article was small, all the effort we put into the project seemed insignificant. So she decided to move on. I, on the other hand, thrive on the highs and lows of this profession. Not knowing what the day will bring seems exciting to me. One 'yes' from an editor, and I'm as happy as a clam.

"If you want a career in media publicity, I would advise you to read, read, read. Study the format of newspapers, watch the twelve, five, six, and ten o'clock news. Read every magazine you can get your hands on and note how things are laid out. Reporters have certain 'beats,' and if you can zero in on what they write about, half the battle is won. Familiarizing oneself with the media is a never-ending responsibility. While there are a few good media guides that provide information, this is not a substitute for studying the style of an individual person, section, or publication. Also, as the media faces the same cutbacks and consolidations as any other industry, changes in personnel happen at a rapid pace.

"If you don't want to go through the trial-and-error process as much as I did, try to get an internship with a PR company. I have used graduate students from the Medill School of Journalism at Northwestern University as freelancers several times. Just remember that in order to make it in this field, you need a good imagination and the ability to find an 'angle.'

"I can't tell you how many times a client has said, 'I do a better job than anyone else in town, and I truly care about my customers.' That's very nice, but it's *boring!* Find out why the client does a better job. What does he or she do differently? Is the business owner an interesting person? What are his or her hobbies? The list goes on and on. You must be able to pick someone's brain until something newsworthy pops out. Then, you must learn who might be fascinated with your information—so much so, that they want to inform their readers about it or share it with the television audience.

"As I look back over the weeks, months, and years, I feel that the most rewarding part of my effort is the knowledge that I have truly made a difference in my client's businesses and, consequently, in their lives. The wide diversity of my clientele makes for a job that never gets boring. And when I look ahead, more than anything else, I wonder what my next project will be."

Fund-Raisers

HELP WANTED: SPECIAL EVENT COORDINATOR

We are seeking an outgoing and polished individual to join our high-profile fund-raising group. This individual will coordinate day-to-day activities related to major special fund-raising events. Duties include organizing special events, generating reports, maintaining databases and other records, and tracking special event expenses. In addition, you will create collateral materials and write various communication pieces. The successful incumbent must be an organized, proactive thinker who enjoys interacting with diverse personalities. Excellent verbal and written communication skills and interpersonal skills are essential. A background in special events and/or arts management experience, including budget administration and communications/meeting management activities is extremely desirable, as is familiarity with desktop publishing software. In return, we offer a stimulating work environment, a competitive benefits package, and the opportunity to advance your career with a performing arts leader. Qualified candidates are requested to forward a confidential resume/salary history immediately.

Job Settings

Fund-raisers are directly involved in planning and organizing programs designed to raise money for colleges; hospitals; political campaigns; and educational, historical, community, religious, arts, cultural, educational, social service, health, advocacy, political, trade, scientific, and research organizations. Also included are youth leadership and other charitable causes. Sometimes referred to as philanthropy, this industry ranks as one of the ten largest industries in the United States.

Fund-raisers are usually asked to determine the length and scope of each campaign; write slogans or other phrases associated with the effort; decide how funds will be solicited; and assign people to carry out these tasks. Then they oversee the efforts to make sure things stay on schedule and go according to plan. They regularly assess and reassess the campaign to make sure that what changes may be needed are made.

Using enthusiasm, energy, and competence, fund-raisers combine skills in financial management, public relations, marketing, accounting, human resources, personnel management, and media communications. Assessing the viability of charitable programs, they devise strategies for meeting goals, identify potential donors, and solicit funds efficiently and effectively. In the 1990s alone, Americans contributed more than $100 billion to educational, health, research, arts, religious, and social welfare organizations.

Fund-raisers may be known by any of the following job titles:

Director of Major Donor Development

Director of Annual Giving

Director of Major Gifts

Development Director

Director of Development

Vice President for Development

Sponsorship Director

Director of Resource Development

Fund-Raising CEO

Fund-Raising Coordinator

Fund-Raising Researcher

Membership Director

Development Research Coordinator

Fund-Raising Director of Development

Fund-raisers fall into one of three general categories. The first group consists of staff members of health centers, social service agencies, community groups, nonprofit organizations, and cultural institutions. In each case, they plan and work on all fund-raising projects. For instance, a fund-raiser who is employed by a college may write to large corporations to solicit contributions.

The second group of fund-raisers works for fund-raising consulting firms. These individuals provide advice to nonprofit organizations about the best ways to raise and manage the money they accumulate. For instance, a hospital that is interested in raising money might hire the services of a consulting firm.

The third group of fund-raisers works for companies that specialize in offering fund-raising events for any organization that wishes to raise money. This, for instance, might include carnivals, concerts, and theater parties.

Fund-raisers often work in temporary locations. They constantly attend meetings, present talks, and meet with volunteers. As the campaign progresses, tension grows and the pace becomes increasingly hectic. With the stress of meeting financial goals within a limited time period, fund-raisers often need to work long hours—perhaps seven-day weeks—in order to meet the designated goals.

Qualifications and Training

Most fund-raisers have liberal arts degrees, though the degree specialty will vary and different organizations may require specific qualifications. If you know in advance that you wish to do fund-raising for an environmental concern, for example, then it would be best to focus on a degree in something related, like environmental studies.

Marketing degrees are also helpful, as is practical knowledge gained in courses such as mathematics, economics, computers, bookkeeping, and accounting. Other suggested courses include psychology, education, speech, sociology, public relations, social work, math, journalism, and business administration.

Individuals considering entering this line of work should have high communication and numerical skills and be well organized and flexible. They must also have the ability to work well with others, work under pressure, and meet deadlines. Fund-raisers must possess excellent selling techniques and need to be excellent motivators.

Computer skills are necessary. In particular, familiarity with some of the special software programs such as Raiser's Edge, Fundmaster, and Donor II is advantageous.

Most employers seek individuals with two to seven years of experience. Internships and volunteer opportunities are ways to get experience, and nonprofits have many more volunteer opportunities than business or government jobs. After gaining five years of experience, you may choose to become certified by the National Society of Fund Raising Executives (NSFRE).

Even though public relations is a relatively new and smaller field, there are more than sixteen thousand professionals working in this field in the United States alone.

Salaries

Earnings for fund-raisers range from volunteers who work for nothing to those who earn a high income—perhaps $200,000 per year or more. A shortage of skilled personnel in this field has prompted some fund-raising counseling firms to offer performance bonuses. Here are some average yearly salaries:

Entry-level fund-raiser director—$26,000

Senior-level director—$44,556

Average fund-raiser in the Northeast—$560 weekly

Average fund-raiser in the Northwest—$380 weekly

Qualified fund-raisers are in high demand. Since the federal government has cut back on spending in the area of social programs, the burden of charitable activity has been thrust upon philanthropic sources.

Words from the Pros

Meet Thomas L. Campbell, Certified Fund-Raising Executive

Thomas Campbell earned his bachelor of science degree in business administration in 1981 and a master of science degree in physical education in 1987 from the University of Delaware. He also received a master of science degree in business administration from Wilkes University in 1990.

He is a Certified Fund-Raising Executive from the National Society of Fundraising Executives and serves as director of development and alumni relations at Allentown College of St. Francis de Sales in Center Valley, Pennsylvania.

"My career here actually began in 1988," he says. "Previously I had worked in Jacksonville, Florida, as a sales and operations manager, but my wife and I were interested in moving back north. I came to Allentown College, thinking it would serve as an excellent practice interview. To my surprise, I was offered the job! I decided to accept it and stay here for a few years. Here it is, eleven years later, and I am still here! Why? Because I love the position!

"Since I had always worked in sales, the work involved was really not that dissimilar. I found that fund-raising was just another version of sales but with a wonderful twist. The work was now affecting students' lives. I know that without the money I raise, many of our students just wouldn't be able to attend college. And since I recognize the value of a college education and the impact it can have on someone's life, I am very motivated to do this kind of work.

"There are no days that are typical. The overriding object is to raise money, of course, but there are lots of steps. You just don't call someone up and expect them to give you money. It's all about building relationships, cultivating people, and identifying potential donors.

"This kind of work brings much joy and is very fulfilling. I would say that the most difficult aspect of this position is that, after eleven years, it is sometimes difficult to rise to the challenge of exceeding the previous years' performance.

"I would advise others who are interested in entering this career to first secure another type of job on the corporate side. With that kind of experience to your credit, you are a much stronger fund-raiser because you understand what executives must deal with and what they are up against."

For More Information

The following list includes professional associations and directories that can aid in your job search. Many of the publications are available in public libraries.

American Marketing Association
250 South Wacker Drive
Chicago, IL 60606

The American Marketing Association is a professional society of marketing and market research executives, sales and promotion managers, advertising specialists, academics, and others interested in marketing. The association sponsors research, seminars, conferences, and student marketing clubs and provides a placement service. It also offers a certification program for marketing managers. The association publishes the *Journal of Marketing*, *Journal of Marketing Research*, *Journal of Health Care Marketing*, and an international membership directory.

National Council for Marketing and Public Relations
364 North Wyndham Avenue
Greely, CO 80634

Members of the National Council for Marketing and Public Relations are communications specialists working within community colleges in areas including alumni, community, government, media, public relations, marketing, publications, and special events. The association works to foster improved relations between two-year colleges and their communities. The council holds an annual conference with exhibits, national surveys, and needs assessment and publishes a journal called *Counsel*.

Additional information can be obtained by contacting:

National Society of Fund Raising Executives (NSFRE)
1101 King Street, Suite 700
Alexandria, VA 22314

American Association of Fund-Raising Counsel and American Association of Fund-Raising Executives
25 West Forty-third Street, Suite 1519
New York, NY 10036

Association for Healthcare Philanthropy
313 Park Avenue, Suite 400
Falls Church, Virginia 22046

Direct Mail Fund Raisers Association
445 West Forty-fifth Street
New York, NY 10036

National Easter Seal Society
230 West Monroe, Suite 1800
Chicago, IL 60606

CHAPTER THREE

Careers in Marketing and Advertising

Promise, large promise, is the soul of an advertisement.
SAMUEL JOHNSON

HELP WANTED: BRAND MARKETING MANAGERS
A leading New York–based confectionery company is seeking results-oriented creative thinkers to be responsible for fueling profitable growth. You will lead the strategic and tactical execution for the retail, mail order, and market sales channels; develop strategies, objectives, and tactics to maximize retail profit and loss performance; and execute annual marketing plan. Conducting and analyzing consumer research, you will execute all aspects of developing new products, develop new merchandising approaches to maximize product shelf impact, and lead consumer communication, including advertising, consumer promotions, and public relations.

Qualified candidates must possess three or more years of experience in a consumer packaged goods/retail environment with experience in hands-on product development and construction of annual marketing, product line. and/or store merchandising plans. A college degree is required; M.B.A. preferred. Interested parties please send resume and salary history to us immediately.

Is the above ad of interest to you? Do you enjoy the prospect of helping companies to determine what the needs and desires of the public really are? If so, you might want to consider a career in marketing or advertising!

Marketing Professionals

There is no mistaking the goal of marketing. It is to reach the consumer and to motivate or persuade a potential buyer; to sell a product, service, idea, or cause; to gain political support; or to influence public opinion.

Firms need to market their products or services profitably. To do so, an overall marketing policy must be established, including product development, market research, market strategies, sales approaches, advertising outlets, promotion possibilities, and effective pricing and packaging.

The Role of the Marketer

Simply stated, marketers try to figure out what consumers have a need for, and salespeople try to encourage people to buy what they are selling. Marketers start at the beginning of the cycle by looking at potential customers and asking themselves, "What do they need?" Once that is determined, marketers look at their companies and ask themselves, "Do we know how to produce it, and can we make money doing it?"

Marketing executives determine the demand for products and services offered by the firm and identify potential consumers, including business firms, wholesalers, retailers, government, or the general public. Mass markets are further categorized according to various factors such as region, age, income, and lifestyle.

In small firms, all marketing responsibilities may be assumed by the owner or chief executive officer. In large firms, which may offer numerous products and services nationally or even worldwide, experienced professionals work together to coordinate these and related activities.

Step by Step

Once marketers come up with product ideas that may have originated from talking to customers or been generated during brainstorming sessions, they begin communicating with product development departments. In some industries, these might be scientists or engineers. They form a team that includes marketing management, marketing researchers, engineers, advertisers, financial advisors, and, eventually, salespeople.

First the team must decide if the product idea is something the customers really want. This is called market research. Market researchers set up focus groups, bringing a group of consumers together and talking to them, finding out what isn't working in their present environments and what they truly need.

Professionals working in market research departments are tuned in to the consumer—what he or she worries about, desires, thinks, believes, and holds dear. Market researchers conduct surveys or one-on-one interviews, utilize existing research, test consumer reactions to new products or advertising copy, track sales figures and buying trends, and become overall experts on consumer behavior. Marketing research assistants report directly to a research executive and are responsible for compiling and interpreting data and monitoring the progress of research projects.

Agency research departments can design questionnaires or other methods of studying groups of people, implement the surveys, and interpret the results. Sometimes research departments hire an outside market research firm to take over some of the workload. For example, a market researcher could come up with a procedure to test the public's reaction to a television commercial; the outside firm would put the procedure into action.

After the market research is conducted, marketers attempt to quantify that need in the marketplace. If thirty people have said they need a particular device, it suggests a strong need, but the company can't afford to build something for just thirty people. It wants to make sure that enough people out there are willing to buy the product. This sparks another round of research.

With successful research results, the concept development stage begins. This is the development of a word or paragraph that describes the product. In some instances, marketers then take that to engineers who develop a prototype.

The prototype is taken to the marketplace for testing and evaluations. With feedback in hand, the team begins to make product improvements.

Once the company is at least 95 percent sure this is the product people want, it's given a final test in the marketplace. The team also tests for claims. For example, a company might want to claim that its new hospital bed will prevent skin sores, but it needs to be able to document that claim.

If all test results point to being able to move forward, the engineers start figuring out how to mass produce the product and marketers plan how their companies can make money on it. For that, they have to look at the production costs and how much customers would be willing to pay for it. One of the big misconceptions in this area is that you take the cost and add a profit percentage to it. Cost is not determined that way. It is generally determined by what people are willing to pay.

The next step is promotion planning. Now that the company has a product, it has to find a way to get the word out. The appropriate team members make brochures and design advertising. At the same time, the numbers are being crunched and production schedules are set up. Marketing experts need to know how fast the product can be made, how quickly it can get out into the field, how many will be bought, and how big the profit will be.

Once a date is set for introducing the product, the sales force is brought in and taught how to present it. Then the product is monitored to see if it's meeting its sale projections. If the product isn't making the projected numbers, top management wants to know why and what is being done about it. Often, though, even if it is making the numbers, top management still wants to know why. That's the way it goes in a competitive business.

Job Settings

Marketing professionals are found in virtually every industry including motor vehicle dealers, printing and publishing firms, department stores, computer and data processing services firms, management and public relations firms, and advertising agencies.

Because marketers and advertising professionals work hand in hand, many marketing departments are located within corporate advertising departments or within private advertising agencies. Private marketing firms function similarly to advertising agencies and work toward the same goals—identifying and targeting specific audiences that will be receptive to specific products, services, or ideas.

Experts advise that individuals start the job search before they near graduation. Those who arrange internships for themselves have an edge; they've already become familiar faces on the job. When an opening comes up, a known commodity (who performed well during the internship) is going to be chosen over an unknown one.

Marketers work long hours, often including evenings and weekends. Working under pressure is unavoidable as schedules change, problems arise, and deadlines and goals must be met.

Marketing managers meet frequently with other managers; some meet with the public and government officials. Substantial travel may be involved. For example, attendance at meetings sponsored by associations or industries is often mandatory.

The Downsides

Although marketing is considered by many to be a "step up" from sales, there's a downside to it. If the company is not making the expected profit, marketers could easily lose their jobs. Their responsibilities for sales volume and profit are the same that salespeople must meet.

In essence, marketers make an agreement with sales departments and personnel. For example, they reason, 'OK, we are

going to sell a hundred units of X product to a particular customer.' But if they spend too much money in product development or advertising and then sell only ninety units, though the
salesperson has the first responsibility, the marketing person is
also responsible. He or she had agreed on what could be sold on
specific advertising and on setting a certain price. If the mark is
missed, it's the marketer's job that is also on the line.

Another downside is that marketers usually supervise salespeople, but the sales force often makes more money than the
marketers do—possibly a lot more money. But to make up for it,
marketers usually also receive good pension plans and bonuses.

Qualifications and Training

A wide range of educational backgrounds are suitable for entry
into marketing jobs, but many employers prefer a broad liberal
arts background. A bachelor's degree in sociology, psychology,
literature, or philosophy, among other subjects, is acceptable.
Familiarity with computerized word processing and database
applications is also important. However, requirements vary
depending upon the particular job.

Most marketing positions are filled by promoting experienced
sales and technical personnel—such as sales representatives,
purchasing agents, buyers, product or brand specialists, advertising
specialists, promotion specialists, or public relations specialists.

The best marketers have a dual background, including sales
experience and a formal education—ideally an M.B.A. Some
start off in sales, then after they've been on the job for a while,
they go back to school for their master's before moving into
marketing.

For marketing management positions, some employers prefer
bachelor's or master's degrees in business administration with
an emphasis on marketing. Courses in business law, economics,
accounting, finance, mathematics, statistics, and psychology are
also recommended.

In highly technical industries, such as computer and electronics manufacturing, bachelor's degrees in engineering or science, combined with master's degrees in business administration, may be preferred.

People interested in becoming marketing managers should be mature, creative, highly motivated, resistant to stress, and flexible, yet decisive. The ability to communicate persuasively, both orally and in writing, with other managers, staff, and the public is vital. Marketing managers also need tact, good judgment, and exceptional ability to establish and maintain effective personal relationships with supervisory and professional staff members and client firms.

Getting Ahead

Because of the importance and high visibility of their jobs, marketing personnel are often prime candidates for advancement. Well-trained, experienced, successful managers may be promoted to higher positions in their own or other firms. Some become top executives. Managers with extensive experience and sufficient capital may open their own businesses. In small firms, where the number of positions is limited, advancement to a management position may come slowly. In large firms, promotion may occur more quickly.

Although experience, ability, and leadership are emphasized for promotion, advancement may be accelerated by participation in management training programs. Many firms also provide their employees with continuing education opportunities, either in-house or at local colleges and universities, and encourage employee participation in seminars and conferences, often provided by professional societies.

Numerous marketing and related associations sponsor national or local management training programs, often in collaboration with colleges and universities. Courses include brand and product management, international marketing, sales management evaluation, telemarketing and direct sales, promotion, marketing communication, market research, organizational communication, and data processing systems procedures and management. Many firms pay all or part of the cost for those who successfully complete courses.

Some associations offer certification programs for marketing managers. This is a plus because certification is a sign of competence and achievement in this field. While relatively few marketing managers currently are certified, the number of managers who seek certification is expected to grow. For example, Sales and Marketing Executives International offers a management certification program based on education and job performance. The American Marketing Association is developing a certification program for marketing managers.

Salaries

According to the most recent National Association of Colleges and Employers survey, starting salaries for marketing majors average about $29,000.

The median annual salary of marketing managers is about $46,000, with the lowest 10 percent earning $23,000 or less and the top 10 percent earning $97,000 or more. Many earn bonuses equal to 10 percent or more of their salaries.

Surveys show that salary levels vary substantially depending upon the level of managerial responsibility, length of service, education, and the employer's size, location, and industry. For example, manufacturing firms generally pay marketing managers higher salaries than nonmanufacturing firms.

According to a recent survey by *Advertising Age* magazine, the average annual salary of a vice president in marketing is $133,000. Other surveys show a variation from $25,000 to $250,000 for marketing managers, depending on the level of education, experience, industry, and the number of employees he or she supervises.

Advertising

"The breakfast of champions." "Where's the beef?" "When it rains, it pours." Such phrases are familiar to most of us because of the effective work that advertising specialists have been performing for years. Some consider this phenomenon a nuisance that interrupts television programming and encourages people to buy products that may or may not be useful. Others look upon it as a great public service. A dominating force in our society, mass-media advertising is a multimillion dollar industry dating back to the invention of movable type in the mid-1400s.

Job Settings

Virtually every type of business makes use of advertising in some form, often through the services of an advertising agency. The American Association of Advertising Agencies defines an advertising agency as "a service company that earns its income from planning, creating, producing, and placing printed advertisements and broadcast commercials for its clients." Agencies may also offer additional services, such as market research, sales promotion, television programming, and public relations.

Agencies that handle many kinds of advertising are called full-service advertising agencies. Other, more specialized agencies, may handle only one area, such as direct marketing.

An advertising agency may consist of only one employee or perhaps several thousand. Salaries will tend to be higher for those employed at bigger full-service agencies, because plum accounts such as IBM or Pepsi Cola are more likely to engage larger advertising agencies.

Many people think the world of advertising is glamorous and exciting—and certain aspects can be. However, as Karen Cole Winters explains in *Your Career in Advertising,* "If you go into advertising expecting a constant whirl of fun and excitement, you'll probably be disappointed."

The work at each agency is frequently divided among several individuals or departments, usually including the following:

- *Account executives* make sure that clients' work is completed satisfactorily and on time. Account executives must be savvy about their agencies and aware of each client's desires and needs. Their responsibilities lie more in the business arena than in the creative aspects of the business.

- *Art directors* must be able to effectively present themes or ideas in convincing visual form through illustration, color, photography, or cinematography.

- *Creative directors* supervise all employees and oversee all activities in the agency. At the top of the hierarchy, creative directors must be innovative and possess solid people skills and business acuity.

- *Researchers* determine what kind of audience would be interested in a particular product or service, why they are interested in the product, and how the public is reacting to advertising campaigns already in place.

- *Media people* ensure that commercials are aired on radio and television and that ads get into magazines and newspapers.

Other advertising positions include television producers, print production managers, graphic artists, illustrators, photographers, freelance writers, print production personnel, traffic managers, and copywriters.

Advertising copywriters are the real creative force behind advertising campaigns. They are the ones who dream up the words for commercials and advertisements and develop the themes for advertising campaigns. Copywriters may also be responsible for creating articles about products or services, sales promotion materials, public relations items, billboards, and promotional brochures.

Copywriters usually begin their work by meeting with the client and/or account executive. After gathering as much information as possible, they let their imaginations flow while looking for a slant on why a product or service is different from all others of its kind. Then they proceed to launch a new advertising campaign with their innovative ideas.

Qualifications and Training

Most employers expect applicants to have college degrees. For those who aspire to become account executives, earning an M.B.A. is especially important. Many schools offer programs in advertising, and a number of top advertising agencies offer in-house training programs for copywriters and account managers.

Since copywriters deal with a wide cross section of ideas and concepts, a general liberal arts background in combination with business is particularly valued. Courses in such subjects as economics, history, journalism, marketing, advertising, math, social sciences, speech, literature, business administration, human relations, and creative writing are recommended.

Copywriters need the skills that all writers should have, including the ability to produce clear, concise prose. Therefore, writing articles, participating in school or church publications, working for local newspapers or radio or television studios, and completing internships are all worthwhile endeavors.

Candidates should prepare a portfolio containing three ads from two or three previous advertising campaigns. These can be class assignments or real ads from actual clients. If they have no advertising experience at all, they can present potential employers with samples of published writing.

Salaries

There is a considerable range of salaries in this field, particularly in different regions of the country. The median annual salary in advertising agencies is about $35,000. Junior copywriters may start out with as little as $15,000; writers with senior status may earn $50,000 to $100,000 and even more as creative directors.

The larger the agency or account, the higher the salary will be. The best locations for jobs are in large cities, such as New York, Chicago, Detroit, Boston, Atlanta, Dallas, Minneapolis, and Los Angeles.

Words from the Pros

Meet Edward Pitkoff, Marketing, Advertising, and Sales Professional

Edward Pitkoff, of Omaha, Nebraska, attended the Philadelphia Museum School of Art, the Pennsylvania Academy of Fine Arts, Temple University, and the Studio School of Art and Design, all in Philadelphia. He also attended a wide variety of marketing and advertising seminars and the School of Visual Arts in New York for a course in television production and direction. He has held several high-ranking positions in marketing, advertising, and sales and is founder and president of Creative Decisions of New York.

"My career began in 1961," says Pitkoff. "After twelve years in positions of designer, assistant art director, art director, and creative director, a freelance business presented itself, and I formed Ed Pitkoff Studios. Ed Pitkoff expanded and evolved into Creative Decisions in 1973, and there the story truly began.

"The idea of doing high-quality, creative advertising that could convince a consumer to purchase a product was attractive to me," Pitkoff explains. "Early on, I was profoundly affected by having a mentor who taught me how to marry the communication to the consumer. I was taught that it is vital for buyers to be able to visualize themselves as part of the product. This is a dictum that has guided me in my longtime work in this field.

"Don't ever become distracted," advises Pitkoff. "Always keep your focus on the business of advertising. And remember—what *you* might want to say to sell this product or service really isn't important. The only thing that *is* important is what would be compelling to consumers. What do they want to hear? What do they want to buy? Ultimately, it is the consumer who is the judge of how well your message has come across. If the product sells, then you know your focused communication has reached its audience."

Meet Cliff Allen, Advertising and Public Relations Company Owner

Cliff Allen is the owner and president of Allen Interactive, an advertising and public relations firm in North Carolina that serves high-tech companies. The firm works with software and hardware companies, from small start-up companies to Microsoft and IBM. Cliff began college by working towards an engineering degree but soon switched to business and later earned a bachelor of arts in marketing from the University of Tulsa in Oklahoma. He is the coauthor of two publications, *Web Catalogue Cookbook* and *Internet World Guide to One-to-One Web Marketing*.

"While in engineering school, I became attracted to computers," Allen says. "Then after working in radio and television for nine years, I caught the 'entrepreneurial bug' and started a software company designed to analyze radio and television ratings data. Although the business was not a huge success, I did learn a great deal about what was called remote computing (using dial-up modems to connect to a remote mainframe).

"For the next thirteen years, I was involved in software development, sales, and marketing of remote computing services working for companies such as United Telecom and General

Electric. This helped me understand the technical side of what is now called the Internet.

"In 1986, I started my present company under the name Allen Marketing Group as an advertising and public relations firm to help software, hardware, and data communications companies with their marketing needs. A few years ago, when we began focusing on the Web, we changed the name to Allen Interactive.

"In 1989, my son spent a summer working in a government facility. After college, he was able to teach our organization how to develop websites, which led us to focus on developing websites for a wide range of companies.

"Until I recently reorganized the company, I had been spending much of my day helping my staff stay current with the skills and knowledge they need to keep up with the changing Internet environment. I was also spending a significant amount of time in sales activities and seeking out new projects. The rest of my time was spent in administrative functions and working directly with clients. Since my time was best spent working directly with clients, and the type of Web projects has changed considerably in the last year, I have reorganized with fewer employees and a set-up that allows all of us to work independently from our own homes. Although we're just completing the transition, it has improved both morale and the quality of our work.

"As with most executives in the Internet industry, I work about fifty to sixty hours per week. Of course, for me, working with the Internet is enjoyable, and part of my time on the Net is just for fun.

"It's a great feeling to share what I've learned about how to use the Internet to achieve a set of goals. Working directly with clients is very satisfying. Handling administrative functions and providing resources for the organization has its own set of rewards, but I don't find it as rewarding as working with clients.

"I would advise others interested in this field to work for a small company where you can get experience in lots of areas of the industry you've selected. Then I would recommend working for a large company where you can focus on a few areas and become proficient. Read as many trade magazines about your industry as you can. Keep up on the trends and the people who are setting the trends. Meet as many people as you can, both within your company and in the industry. Use a top-notch database to record your contacts. It's always amazing when someone you met years ago calls you out of the blue. You thus need a way to quickly recall information about them. Speak in front of groups whenever possible, whether it's a departmental meeting where you summarize your team's progress or an industry conference. People who stand up and speak are remembered and are seen as experts and leaders."

Meet Dennis Abelson, Advertising, Promotions, and Sales Professional

Dennis Abelson earned a bachelor of arts degree in classical languages from Washington University in St. Louis, Missouri. He subsequently earned a master of science in journalism with a focus on advertising from Northwestern Medill School of Communications in Evanston, Illinois. He has experience as a copywriter, associate creative director, and creative director.

"Ten years ago I was making a substantial living as a freelance writer," he says. "But the isolation and lack of significant, bigger-budget creative challenges was starting to bring me down. Then I was contacted by Don Tomala, my future partner, who had come across one of my promotional mailings. He was in the process of establishing an integrated, full-service marketing, consulting, and communications firm to fill a gap he had experienced as a Fortune 500 sales and marketing director. After a somewhat rocky start (it was the middle of an economic recession and few companies had even heard of integrated marketing), we eventually bootstrapped ourselves into a successful, growing company. A few years ago, Tomala and I disassociated ourselves from a third partner and changed our corporate name from the Figa Group to Matrix Partners.

"Our current client roster comprises a highly eclectic mix of companies, who turn to us for a wide range of services, including packaging, advertising, promotions, direct mail, and sales presentations. In 1997, we became agency of record for Anixter International, a global distributor of computer cabling and networking systems. We also serve the Quaker Oats Continental Coffee Division, the American National Can Flexible Packaging Group, Vitner's Potato Chips, the Dive Equipment and Marketing Association, and MS BioScience, a fast-growing agricultural biotech company.

"I originally got into the creative end of advertising because I couldn't see myself holding down a nine-to-five job. It also gave me the opportunity to keep pursuing my interests in audio engineering and cartooning. In my undergraduate years, I was program director of the campus radio station as well as the creator of a weekly comic strip in the campus paper.

"There is no typical day in this industry. Perhaps that is what attracts so many people. But it might unfold somewhat like this:

8 to 9 A.M.—Revise ad copy, circulate for internal review.

9 to 10 A.M.—Attend project status meetings and review logistics and costs to date.

10 to 10:30 A.M.—Finalize ad copy, fax to client.

10:30 to 11 A.M.—Review logo designs and alternate color treatments for new brand.

11 to 12 P.M.—Perform on-line trademark search for proposed theme line.

12 to 1 P.M.—Eat lunch while drafting new presentation.

1 to 1:30 P.M.—Call client regarding new promotion.

1:30 to 4 P.M.—Conceptualize with designer and writer on direct mail project.

4 to 4:30 P.M.—Have meeting to refine thinking on new business presentation.

4:30 to 5 P.M.—Edit PC-based presentation for biotech client.

5 to 6 P.M.—Finalize new business presentation.

6 to 7 P.M.—Continue conceptualizing on direct mail project, take home to finish.

9 to 11 P.M.—Finish writing direct mailer.

"What does it mean to be doing my kind of work?" asks Abelson. "At times it seems totally thankless, but, on the other hand, what other profession pays you to legally hallucinate and play creatively with concepts and pictures?

"Here is my list of upsides:

- No time for corporate politics or hidden agendas

- The opportunity to be familiar with more than a hundred different industries

- The satisfaction of contributing visibly and dramatically to the success of a client's business

"And here are some of the downsides:

- The hours

- Certain clients, who shall remain nameless

- Certain clients who play it safe when they should be more competitive

- Logistical and budgetary constraints on creativity

"I would tell others who are considering a career in advertising and marketing to start with the largest organization that will hire you. And be prepared for the long haul."

Meet Jane Ward, Senior Marketing Specialist

Jane Ward received a bachelor of arts degree from Catholic University in Washington, D.C. She majored in English with minors in French and philosophy. She later earned a master of philosophy degree in Irish Literature from Trinity College in Dublin, Ireland.

"I came back to the United States from Ireland in 1995," she says, "and had a difficult time finding a job. I found that a master's degree in Irish Literature is actually a handicap in the job market, particularly if you don't have much work experience. So I learned Web publishing—HTML conversion, layout, and so forth—and found a well-paying job that utilized these skills. Unfortunately, I found this work very boring and was only biding my time until I could get a more interesting job. In the meantime, I was promoted twice at the Web publishing job, proving to potential employers that I could manage well in a professional environment.

"When a job as a marketing specialist came up at a software company, it was a perfect fit. I had proven that I could learn the technical aspects of a job, and I provided my employers with some writing samples. So, since 1997 I have been creating public relations and marketing materials for that software company. I now hold the position of senior marketing specialist.

"I write website content and manage the site by supervising the graphic designers and approving graphics to go on the Web. I am in charge of press releases and ad copy, and I supervise the production of the ads. I also go to about six or seven trade shows per year, staffing the booth or speaking to the press about our company. I also help with product documentation by editing for style and grammar, though I don't do technical writing, per se.

"I work about fifty hours each week. And since I recently switched from a PC to a laptop, I have been able to bring work home with me. This is both good and bad, I've found. It provides a convenience, but sometimes I feel as if work has invaded my home life too much.

"I'm very busy, but the work environment is pretty relaxed with a very deliberate casualness. In software, people often wear very casual clothes and look down on typical corporate types who wear suits and work in the big city. Also, software, as an industry, is still very young. This is evidenced by the fact that the average age of people working for my company is probably less than thirty years.

"I enjoy writing a piece, a press release for example, and then seeing it picked up and published by a magazine. It gives me a thrill to see such immediate results from my work. But I don't like going to trade shows because I don't enjoy traveling and having to spend time away from my family. Also, that can get pretty tedious. However, I do understand that it's important for our company to be seen at important shows.

"To individuals who are considering this type of career, I would recommend learning how to start looking at the world around you with a critical eye. When an ad comes on television, pay attention to it . What was the goal of the people who created it? Who is their target market? What elements did they pull together to create the ad?

"Since I am involved in the writing end of marketing, I would recommend that you learn how to truly write well. I've seen so many graduates—even those of Ivy League schools—who can't write a complete sentence. And I strongly recommend a liberal arts education, which teaches you how to think and how to artic-ulate your thoughts. These are the kinds of tools that you need to achieve success in any industry."

Meet George DiDomizio, Advertising and Trademark Specialist

George DiDomizio is currently self-employed as president of Gemini Trademark Services in Pennsylvania. He earned a bachelor of business administration degree from Ursinus College of Pennsylvania after attending night school for ten years.

"After a thirty-five year career, mostly in advertising, I began Gemini Trademark Services in 1992, the year after I retired from Merck and Company," DiDomizio recalls. "During my many years with Merck, I devoted part of my time to trademark issues. In fact, my very first report during my market research assignments dealt with physician preferences for pharmaceutical trademarks. I didn't know at that time how important trademarks would become in my personal and professional life. The date of the report was March 15, 1963. Some ten years later, I was asked to serve on the Merck Trademark Committee. Part of the assignment was to participate in brainstorming sessions in an effort to come up with trademarks for our products. I enjoyed the process of 'making up language,' and colleagues told me I had a knack for coming up with interesting and useful names.

"When I was promoted to director of creative services in 1975, I was also asked to assume the role of chairperson of the Merck Trademark Committee. The trademark function was considered an addition to my regular advertising duties, which involved supervising an internal team of about thirty people and a group of about fifty outside agencies, design shops, film producers, and various other communication firms.

"I gave a lot of attention to the trademark function, in part because a trademark has such durability. Advertising campaigns, slogans, logos, and visuals have a limited life span, but a trademark, if properly cared for, lasts forever. And, unlike slogans and themes that wear out with use, a trademark grows more powerful and valuable with use. That was exciting for me. During my time at Merck, I was fortunate to give names to many of the company's most famous products. As this is being written, the world's largest-selling product is Zocor, a name that I coined while at Merck.

"Among the daily thrills for me is to see one of my trademarks on television or in print or hear it on the radio. One of my all-time favorites is to hear Paul Harvey do a commercial for Pepcid AC, another of my trademarks. He has such a resonance to his voice that it makes words sound important and impressive.

"Probably the most important influence on my trademark work is songwriting. I was fortunate to be one of the founding members of SONA, Songwriters of North America. SONA is mainly interested in helping amateur songwriters get thoughts on paper and take whatever additional steps are needed to get the song into print, obtain air time, interest the press, and so forth. I often tell clients that making up trademarks is a little like writing songs. Both activities pack a lot of message into a few words—or a few letters in the case of trademarks. Both a song and a trademark have the potential to become embedded in people's minds. Both a song and a trademark can evoke emotions.

"I like to think of the job as playing with the alphabet. To come up with the six or seven letters that might become a famous trademark requires a lot of effort, not unlike mining for gold. Most trademark projects involve long lists of potential candidates, sometimes as many as a thousand or more. The lists are created through a variety of techniques including brainstorming sessions and computer software programs.

"I like to work with a creative technique I call 'brain writing' that involves a group of six to fifteen people silently building on each other's ideas. We have a special form that participants use to enter their ideas for trademarks in a burst of three at a time. The form is passed along to another person, who is asked to build on the first three names or use any portion of the suggestions to come up with entirely new approaches. In a typical session of about thirty minutes, each person can generate about fifty candidates.

"I have a software program called GENIX that I also use to generate trademarks candidates. The program is quite sophisticated and permits me to take word fragments, called phonemes, and combine them in an almost infinite variety of ways. GENIX can generate words at random or can take an existing prefix and add a variety of suffixes. It can hold a suffix and add a variety of prefixes. The easy part is building long lists of names. The hard part is sorting through the lists to find the linguistic gold.

"The creative part of the job takes about half of my time. Another 20 to 30 percent of my time is spent on the legal aspects. That is, I need to be sure that names of interest are not already taken by others. As this is being written, there are more than a hundred thousand trademarks on file at the U.S. Patent and Trademark Office in Class 5, the area devoted to pharmaceutical and related products. Since most of my clients are interested in global trademarks, the legal screening and searching is done on a global basis. There are more than one million trademarks on file in various countries around the world.

"Using creative magic to generate the sequence of letters that forms a new word and meets the project criteria, then getting a legal green light for global availability is like hitting a grand slam home run.

"A typical day for me begins with a walk with Sabrina, my Labrador retriever, who I refer to as my director of security. Our walks take us through sixteen heavily wooded acres that surround my home and office. During these walks, I am often fortunate enough to get insights and ideas on how to deal with the creative or legal challenges facing me. During my days at Merck, I would often refer to a particularly difficult challenge as a 'dog walking problem,' meaning that the only way to come up with a good answer was to literally walk the dog. In those days, the black Labrador retriever was Blaze.

"After the walk, we settle in for calls and contracts in Europe. More often than not, I try to reach my European clients shortly after lunch for them, which is about 7 A.M. here. Currently, I have active clients in France, Germany, and Sweden.

"I try to devote half or more of the morning hours to creative activities, such as building candidate lists, evaluating candidates, screening candidates or various computer databases, and so forth. This is largely a one-person operation, although from time to time, I bring in an attorney to work directly with me on legal searches and opinions. I am pursuing a juris doctor degree from LaSalle University in Louisiana, but until I get the degree and pass the bar, I am unable to render legal advice.

"The balance of the day is spent on conference calls, correspondence, the Internet, and related activities. I try to limit travel to client offices because I find it is unnecessary. Once a project is underway, most of the progress can be readily handled via conference calls. I have video conference capability on my computer, but except for some test use, I have not made it part of my business routine.

"The most enjoyable part of this job is creating language. There is a wonderful satisfaction in knowing that a piece of language did not exist until you gave it form. Another positive part of my trademark adventure is being an expert in a very narrow field of commerce. The more difficult the challenge, the better I like it.

"I think that an ideal trademark person is one who knows more about trademark law than any marketing person and more about marketing than any trademark attorney."

For More Information

The following list includes professional associations and directories that can aid in your job search. Many of the publications are available in public libraries.

American Marketing Association
250 South Wacker Drive
Chicago, IL 60606

The American Marketing Association is a professional society of marketing and market research executives, sales and promotion managers, advertising specialists, academics, and others interested in marketing. The association fosters research, sponsors seminars, conferences, and student marketing clubs, and provides a placement service. It also offers a certification program for marketing managers and publishes the *Journal of Marketing; Journal of Marketing Research; Journal of Health Care Marketing;* and an international membership directory.

Magazine Publishing Career Directory
Gale Research, Inc.
P.O. Box 33477
Detroit, MI 48232-5477

National Council for Marketing and Public Relations
364 North Wyndham Avenue
Greeley, CO 80634

Members in the National Council for Marketing and Public Relations are communications specialists working within community colleges in areas including alumni, community, government, media, public relations, marketing, publications, and coordinating special events. The association works to foster improved relations between two-year colleges and their communities. The organization holds an annual conference with exhibits, national surveys, and needs assessment and publishes a journal called *Counsel.*

Additional information can be obtained by contacting:

Sales and Marketing Executives International
458 Statler Office Tower
Cleveland, OH 44115

Sales and Marketing Executives International offers a management certification program.

CHAPTER FOUR

Careers in Politics

Political action is the highest responsibility of a citizen.
JOHN F. KENNEDY

HELP WANTED: FULL-TIME ASSISTANT TO VILLAGE MANAGER

Our small village is seeking an assistant for our busy village manager. We are interested in someone who can handle a variety of projects and details simultaneously. We need an individual with a college degree who has experience and a sustained interest in politics, government, and serving the public.

Does a political job hold some interest for you? Are you attracted to the idea of serving others? Then read on for ideas on how you might find your niche in the world of politics.

Careers in Politics

At the top of the political hierarchy are mayors, governors, supervisors, senators, representatives, and, of course, the president and vice president of the country. All are elected to administer government. They handle all of the business of a city, town, state, county, or the country as a whole. It is their job to pass laws to keep order, to set up special programs to benefit people, and to spend the taxpayers' money on goods and services. As problem solvers, they meet with community leaders to find out the needs of the people, and then they search for ways to meet those needs.

There are many other levels of political careers—all the way down to the local levels. This would include those who work for political change in their neighborhoods as well as those in an official capacity, such as precinct captain. Some of these jobs are voluntary, unpaid positions that could eventually lead to paying positions.

All positions except appointed government managers are elected by their constituents. Non-elected managers are hired by a local government council or commission.

Chief Executives and Legislators

Government chief executives, like their counterparts in the private sector, have overall responsibility for the performance of their organizations. Working in conjunction with legislators, they set goals and then organize programs to attain them. They appoint department heads who oversee the work of the civil servants in charge of carrying out programs and enforcing laws enacted by their legislative bodies. They oversee budgets specifying how government resources will be used and ensure that resources are used properly and programs are carried out as planned.

Routinely, chief executives meet with legislators and constituents to discuss proposed programs and determine their levels of support. They frequently confer with leaders of other governments to solve mutual problems. Sometimes they have to make painful and difficult decisions, such as breaking diplomatic relationships with other countries or even declaring war.

Chief executives nominate citizens to boards and commissions, solicit bids from and select contractors to do work for the government, encourage business investment and economic development in their jurisdictions, and seek federal or state funds. Chief executives of large jurisdictions rely on a staff of aides and assistants, but those in small jurisdictions often must do much of the work themselves.

Legislators are the elected officials who pass or amend laws. They include United States senators and representatives, state senators and representatives, county legislators, and city and town council members.

Legislators may introduce bills in the legislative body and examine and vote on bills introduced by other legislators. They often make decisions on issues such as the types of weapons the country will need for defense, how much money should be spent on the space program, and how to protect the environment. In preparing legislation, they read staff reports and may work with constituents, representatives of interest groups, members of boards and commissions, the chief executive and department heads, and others with an interest in the legislation. They generally must approve budgets and the appointments of department heads and commission members submitted by the chief executive. In some jurisdictions, the legislative body appoints a city, town, or county manager. Many legislators, especially at the state and federal levels, have staff members to perform research, prepare legislation, and help resolve constituents' problems.

Both chief executives and legislators perform many ceremonial duties such as opening new buildings, making proclamations, welcoming visitors, and leading celebrations. It is both a privilege and an important responsibility to serve in public office.

Serving at State or Local Levels

At the state and local levels, individuals may seek the following offices:

Governor

Lt. Governor

Secretary of State

State Senator

State Representative

Attorney General

State Treasurer

Comptroller

County Board President

County Commissioner

Assessor

Board of Tax Appeals

Clerk of the Circuit Court

County Clerk

Recorder of Deeds

Sheriff

State's Attorney

Treasurer

Township Supervisor

Village Manager

Board Secretary/Deputy Village Clerk

Village Board of Trustee

Library and Park District Official

As an example, let's take a look at the Illinois General Assembly. Now in its ninety-first session, the assembly is composed of 59 senators and 118 representatives. Collectively, they are responsible for enacting, amending, or repealing laws; passing resolutions; adopting appropriation bills; and conducting inquiries on proposed legislation. The legislature also acts on amendments to the United States Constitution submitted by Congress, proposes amendments to the Illinois Constitution, and takes responsibility for impeachment and conviction of executive and judicial officeholders in the state.

Many political careerists need to hire complete staffs to help them perform their duties more efficiently. This is an excellent way to gain some experience and some contacts in the political arena. This, in turn, can well provide an open door to a career in politics.

Working Conditions

The working conditions of chief executives and legislators vary with the size and budget of the governmental unit. Time spent at work ranges from meeting once a month for a local council member to sixty or more hours per week for a United States senator.

United States senators and representatives, governors and lieutenant governors, and chief executives and legislators in large local jurisdictions usually work full-time year-round, as do county and city managers. Many state legislators work full-time while legislatures are in session (usually for two to six months a year) and part-time the rest of the year. Local elected officials in many jurisdictions work a schedule that is officially designated part-time but actually is the equivalent of a full-time schedule when unpaid duties are taken into account.

In addition to their regular schedules, chief executives are on call at all hours to handle emergencies. Some jobs require occasional out-of-town travel, but others involve long periods away from home to attend sessions of the legislature. Opportunities for government or political jobs may be found throughout the country.

Qualifications and Training

Voters seek to elect the individual believed to be most qualified from among a number of candidates who meet the minimum age, residency, and citizenship requirements. There are no formal educational requirements for public officeholders. However, successful candidates must be able to show the people that they are qualified for the jobs they seek, and a good education is one of the best qualifications a candidate can offer.

Successful candidates usually have a strong record of accomplishment in paid and unpaid work in their districts. Some have business, teaching, or legal experience; meanwhile, others come from a wide variety of occupations. In addition, many have experience as members of boards or commissions. Some candidates become well known for their work with charities, political action groups, political campaigns, or with religious, fraternal, and social organizations.

Management-level work experience and public service help develop the planning, organizing, negotiating, motivating, fundraising, budgeting, public speaking, and problem-solving skills needed to run an effective political campaign. Candidates must make decisions quickly, sometimes on the basis of limited or contradictory information. They must inspire and motivate their constituents and their staffs. They need to appear sincere and candid and able to present their views thoughtfully and convincingly. Additionally, they must know how to hammer out compromises and satisfy the demands of constituents. National and statewide campaigns require massive amounts of energy and stamina, as well as superior fund-raising skills.

Town, city, and county managers are generally hired by the local council or commission. Managers come from a variety of educational backgrounds. A master's degree in public administration, including courses such as public financial management and legal issues in public administration, is widely recommended. Virtually all town, city, and county managers have at least bachelor's degrees and the majority hold master's degrees. Working in management support positions in government is a prime source for the experience and personal contacts required in eventually securing a manager position.

Generally, a town, city, or county manager in a smaller jurisdiction is required to have expertise in a wide variety of areas. Those who work for larger jurisdictions specialize in financial, administrative, and personnel matters. For all managers, communication skills and the ability to get along with others are essential.

Advancement opportunities for elected public officials are not clearly defined. Because elected positions normally require a period of residency and local public support is critical, officials can usually advance to other offices only in the jurisdictions where they live. For example, council members may run for mayor or for positions in the state government, and state legislators may run for governor or for Congress. Many officials are not overly politically ambitious, however, and do not seek advancement. Others lose their bids for reelection or voluntarily leave the occupation. A lifetime career as a government chief executive or legislator is rare except for those who reach the national level.

Town, city, and county managers have better-defined career paths. They generally obtain master's degrees in public administration, then gain experience as management analysts or assistants in government departments working for committees, councils, or chief executives. They learn about planning, budgeting, civil engineering, and other aspects of running a government. With sufficient experience, they may be hired to manage small governments and often move on to manage progressively larger governments over time.

Salaries

Salaries for public administrators vary widely, depending on the size of the government unit and on whether the job is part-time, full-time and year-round, or full-time for only a few months a year. Salaries range from little or nothing for a small town council member to $200,000 a year for the president of the United States.

According to the International City/County Management Association (ICMA), the average annual salary of chief elected county officials in 1996 was $25,600, while for chief elected city officials it was about $12,200. ICMA data indicate that the average salary for city managers was about $70,600 in 1996, while that of county managers was about $86,700.

According to the National Conference of State Legislatures, the salary for legislators in the forty states that paid an annual salary ranged from about $10,000 to $47,000 per year. In six states, legislators received a daily salary plus an allowance for expenses while legislatures were in session. Two states paid no expenses and only nominal daily salaries, while two states paid no salary at all but did pay a daily expense allowance. Salaries and expense allowances were generally higher in the larger states. Data from *Book of the States, 1996-97,* indicate that gubernatorial annual salaries ranged from $60,000 in Arkansas to $130,000 in New York. In addition to a salary, most governors received perquisites such as transportation and an official residence. In 1997, U.S. senators and representatives earned $133,600, the Senate and House majority and minority leaders $148,400, and the vice president $171,500.

Words from the Pros

Meet Margo Vroman, Assistant City Attorney

Margo Vroman earned her bachelor of science and master of arts degrees from Western Michigan University in Kalamazoo and her juris doctorate from the University of Toledo in Ohio. Presently she is employed by the City of Lansing, Michigan, as assistant city attorney. She is also a part-time adjunct professor at Michigan State University, Detroit College of Law.

"I've been practicing law since 1982 and have been with the city attorney's office since 1997. After trying several different career avenues, I opted for one that combined litigation with appellate practice.

"I had an interest in becoming a lawyer as far back as grade school. I think the movie *To Kill a Mockingbird* had some impact in making me think that law was a profession where integrity and justice were valued. I've always admired people who are willing to fight for what's right even in the face of extreme odds, and it's rewarding to see that sometimes that willingness leads to significant positive change in our society. Now that I'm here, reality has set in, but I still get a good deal of satisfaction when I think I've helped right one small wrong in somebody's life.

"I've always been a lawyer or legal writer, although my professional career has been pretty diverse. After trying private practice and working as a legal editor for a major publisher and the Michigan Supreme Court, I've decided I like a job that combines diverse practice areas with the opportunity to write appellate court briefs.

"Our city attorney's office is divided into criminal and civil divisions. I work in the civil division, where I am chief appellate counsel. That means I work on all the appeals that we file or respond to. For complicated cases, we usually put together a team that I coordinate. Appellate work entails reading the trial court transcripts, researching the legal issues surrounding perceived legal errors, and writing a brief that convinces the higher court that your side should win. This means spending a lot of time in front of the computer and in the law library. It's not particularly stressful unless there are numerous cases with simultaneous deadlines or you know the outcome can cost your client $15 million if you lose.

"I also spend a fair amount of time rendering legal advice to city departments, the mayor's office, and city council. This may involve a written memo or a simple 'I wouldn't do that' when someone grabs you at the lunch counter. My specialty, as far as contracts go, is in the area of software purchase agreements, and I also do most of the other technology-related projects.

"In addition, I litigate civil cases in state and federal court when we can't manage to negotiate an out-of-court settlement. Of course, this means deposing witnesses, obtaining evidence, and preparing all pleadings, in addition to court appearances.

"Sometimes we're extremely busy and it seems like there's no way possible we can get everything done that *has* to be done. Other times we get to slow down, relax a little, and smell a rose or two. Most of the time it's somewhere in between.

"What I like most about my current position is the diversity of things I get to do. I admittedly have a very short attention span and am easily bored. This job is good because I am always learning something new and am sometimes given the opportunity to present new and important legal issues to the Supreme Court. Every now and then, I get to feel like my contribution actually makes a positive difference in the way things work.

"The downside of a position like this is that lawyers and law departments are always everyone's favorite whipping posts. When you tell people they can't legally do what they want to do, their respond by taking it out on the messenger. If they do it anyway and a lawsuit ensues, they blame the law department for not doing a good job. Also, when you work for a government entity you always have to deal with the political ramifications of everything you do (not that this isn't a problem in other environments, too). As if this isn't enough, you also have to deal with the crazies who think it is their God-given right to show up in any governmental office and harass the people working there.

"Of course, some of these incidents can actually break up an otherwise boring day—like the person who barged into my office to tell me that aliens had landed in his backyard, grabbed his mother out of her lawn chair, and whisked her away in their spaceship. After checking into his story (yes, I was worried about what might actually have happened to mom), I learned that his sister had determined he wasn't a very good caregiver for their mother, and she came and got mom and put her in a nursing home.

"I guess I'd suggest that anyone contemplating a law career think it through very carefully. They had better make sure they have thick skin. You don't get many thank-yous in this business, but you do get a lot of blame and name-calling. I would also point out that the cost of a legal education today often outweighs the salary you can expect to earn as a lawyer. I also teach as an adjunct at one of the local law schools, and it's heartbreaking to see young people who have worked so hard to graduate with a job that pays them $32,000 a year when they have student loan payments of more than $500 a month. Still, it's rewarding to know that, as a lawyer, you really can make a difference in this world."

Meet Karen Sweeny-Justice, National Park Service Professional

Karen Sweeny-Justice earned an A.A.S. degree in graphic art from Onondaga Community College in Syracuse, New York; an A.A. in communications from Cazenovia College in Cazenovia, New York; and a B.S. in human development from Syracuse University in New York.

She serves as a national park ranger for interpretation (Big South Fork National River and Recreation Area in Tennessee and Kentucky) and has been associated with the park service for more than twelve years. During that time, she completed a number of courses with the National Park Service and National Career Workshops, including the following: Developing African-American Interpretive Programs, Interpretation for Children, Self-Study Course for Interpreters, Interpretation in Urban Areas, Ranger Skills, How to Supervise People, Management

Skills for Success in the 1990s, How to Work with People, Orientation to the Management of National Park System Resources, and first aid and safety courses.

"After working in a bank as a financial sales counselor for more than two years, I decided I needed a change," she says. "So I quit that job and, sight unseen, accepted a position for a lot less money as a summer employee at the Old Faithful Lodge in Yellowstone National Park. I used the chance to be in the park as a basis for exploration of the region, and, discovering that I was one of the 'older' concession employees (at the ripe old age of twenty-eight), I decided I needed something that would get me out of the dorm. So, when I learned that the park service needed volunteers, I signed on to work at the Old Faithful Visitor Center. The rangers I worked with were informative and trusted me enough to let me solo on explanations of what was going on. I even got good at predicting when Old Faithful would erupt.

"While I still worked at the lodge, the visitor center experience was what led to my future. At Yellowstone, I learned about a group called the Student Conservation Association, and I signed on to volunteer with the group that winter. I was selected by Biscayne National Park and spent the winter down in Florida doing the same work that the seasonal rangers did. That included presenting programs like glass bottom boat tours and staffing the visitor centers.

"Basically I discovered I liked the chance to help visitors better understand the parks they were in. Besides, I've always liked talking to people! Many of the other rangers I know started out as volunteers, so the path I took isn't that unique.

"There was nothing in my past experience that would have indicated that I'd like parks. I grew up in a city and am the only one of my family that has left. And not only have I left my home town, I've traveled and worked in a variety of locations in the past twelve years, including Yellowstone, Biscayne, Shenandoah, Lowell, Valley Forge, and Big South Fork.

"Some parks are busier than others," she explains. "While an urban park like Valley Forge might see more than one thousand visitors on a Saturday, a park in a rural area (that one must really drive to get to) might have fewer than a hundred visitors. Park seasons vary, too. Yellowstone is mostly summer, while the Everglades is mostly winter. It all depends on the weather and natural conditions. Some days it may be boring and slow, allowing lots of time to do research, while on other days one may not even get a chance for lunch.

"Interpretation isn't dangerous, but on occasion, one may be asked to help with medical emergencies and search and rescues," Sweeny-Justice continues. "Some parks have different shifts that need to be covered, and sometimes that means opening or closing buildings alone.

"Forty-hour work weeks are the norm, although if staff is slim, there may be overtime. The atmosphere varies from park to park. And each park does get its share of visitors who think that because rangers are public servants, they can be walked over, ignored, or abused. It doesn't happen often, but it does happen. I've had people shout and yell at me and call me names. On the other hand, I've received lots of praise from people who have enjoyed the programs I've done enough to send letters to my supervisors.

"The upsides of the job are the feelings that come when you can see people grasping concepts they didn't understand before or helping people to make the most of their visits. Getting to see the treasures our nation offers is a benefit, too. It used to be said that rangers were 'paid in sunsets.'

"The downsides are the fact that the pay isn't spectacular, people don't always use their common sense when they're on vacation, and there is a lot of work in buildings that can be very uncomfortable. For example, I worked year-round in Washington's Headquarters at Valley Forge. The building was built in the eighteenth century, didn't have a modern heating or cooling system, and had only one bare lightbulb hanging in the stairwell behind the door to the basement. Needless to say, it wasn't very comfortable.

"Working for the National Park Service can be mentally draining, especially if you want to make it a career. I say this because it is very competitive, and there are no guarantees that permanent employment will come to you. I had to take a job as a permanent secretary to get my status to apply for permanent ranger positions. And as a seasonal employee, you don't get any benefits like insurance and can be let go at any time. Right now, I have a friend who has been working as a temporary employee for more than ten years, and she only knows that she has a job until March. Another friend who has been in a similar situation was very lucky to have competed successfully for her job, and she is now a permanent employee.

"If you don't like speaking to total strangers or giving programs to audiences that range from a few people to crowds of more than a hundred, you wouldn't really enjoy this job. But for those of us who do, it's perfect!"

Meet Vera Marie Badertscher, Political Campaign Manager and Consultant

Vera Marie Badertscher earned a bachelor of arts degree and a bachelor of science degree in education from Ohio State University in 1960. Her major was theater and English. She went on to secure a master of fine arts from Arizona State University in 1976, focusing on theater.

"Originally I served as campaign manager for many years," Badertscher says. "More recently I have been employed as a campaign consultant. I started as a citizen volunteer in city projects," she explains. "As a young mother, I wanted a better library system where I lived in Scottsdale, Arizona, so I volunteered for a committee. There I met officeholders, was invited to serve on their advisory committees, and eventually asked for and received pay for managing a city council election campaign.

"I enjoyed the sense of accomplishment while working in politics—being able to promote my beliefs and make things happen," she says. "I also enjoyed the fact that most people involved in politics are action oriented and optimistic, true believers. My chief asset was an ability to figure out the best way to communicate political messages and move people to action.

"My volunteer work in a federated women's club gave me experience in bringing diverse people together to work on projects, combining government and private energies, communicating, and organizing projects. My theater background helped me focus on short-term, collaborative projects.

"As a campaign manager, I spent most of my time communicating with volunteers—mostly on the phone but sometimes in memos or in newsletters. It is a very intense job because of the limited time for a political campaign (usually about nine months—perhaps symbolic?). Someone advised me when I managed my first congressional campaign that during the last couple of weeks of the campaign I would be making a dozen decisions every hour and one in twenty or so would be truly important.

"Prioritizing is critical in political campaigns," she stresses. "You need to know the difference between decisions that do not affect the outcome (what color the signs are) and decisions that do (whether the candidate shouldattend a particular debate).

"A campaign manager rounds up diverse interest groups, volunteers, the candidate and his or her family, advertising personnel, researchers, and fund-raisers. The key to being successful is keeping the focus on what will get the candidate elected and not allowing anyone in the campaign to draw the focus in another direction. You can expect to talk on the phone all day, check on other people's work, and stay close to the candidate to keep him or her on track. Generally, you are trying to keep costs down, so the work surroundings are on the primitive side—borrowed

furniture and unpainted walls. You can count on noise and constant activity. (If it's quiet, you're probably losing.) This presents
a hard atmosphere to concentrate in, but that's the job.

"A campaign consultant has more luxury of time to think
than does a campaign manager. The consultant typically analyzes
voting data history; studies the candidate, the opponent, and the
voters; and writes a strategic plan for bringing the voters to support that candidate. Some consultants specialize in media or
mail, but I have been a generalist, doing strategy and writing
direct mail. The consultant works in an office or home office and
meets weekly or biweekly with the candidate, the campaign manager, and others involved in the campaign. Once the plan is written, the consultant is available to help with fine-tuning, make
adjustments, review media plans, determine what questions to
ask in polling, and interpret the results. While the campaign
manager's job is not done until the polls close on election day,
the consultant's job is done a few days prior to the election when
no more mail can be sent or advertising launched that will affect
the outcome.

"I most like the ability to work out the puzzles involved in
bringing together the circumstances, the candidate, and the voters in order to persuade them that they will be better off to elect
that candidate. I like the thinking and the communicating of
politics.

"What I least like is having to be nice to a bunch of people
whom I might not particularly like or admire. However, I have
been fortunate in being able to choose the candidates I work for,
so I have worked for people I believe in and personally support.
However, politics is about coalition building, so sometimes the
expression 'politics makes strange bedfellows' is all too true.

"I am frustrated with the general disdain for politics and the
growing cynicism, which I fear will damage our democracy," she
says. "So, I would like to be able to persuade people that there
are good and worthy people in elected office. My hat is truly off

to the people who do participate—by voting or by running for office or by supporting those who run.

"I would advise anyone interested in entering this kind of work to introduce yourself to a candidate you admire and volunteer to help. Political science classes teach theory, but only campaigning teaches campaigning. Don't try to tell the candidate how to run his campaign or volunteer to be the brains behind the organization until you have actually done some of the grunt work of campaigning and learned it from the inside out. You'd be surprised how many people come to a campaign manager and say, 'I'm really good at strategy,' when all the campaign manager really needs is someone to go out in a pickup truck and put up signs. And before any of that—register to vote. Read up on the issues. And last but not least—*vote*."

Meet Wade Hyde, Regional Transportation Board Member and Political Consultant

Wade Hyde earned a bachelor of arts degree in education and history from East Texas State University in Commerce, Texas. He continued his education and received a master of arts degree in urban affairs from the University of Texas at Arlington. He also earned a master of arts degree in civic affairs teaching from the University of Dallas in Irving, Texas. He has served as a volunteer campaign manager consultant, as a volunteer civic board member, and as a planning and zoning commission member in Irving, Texas, for four years. Currently he serves as a member of the regional transportation board and member and officer of the Visiting Nurses Association.

"In 1980, I began volunteering in organizations supporting interests with legislative agendas," he says. "Political events were at the center of what I found most interesting and exciting in earlier years. These events included listening to the presidential nominating conventions (before pollsters and analysts took all the fun and suspense out of final outcomes) on the radio and waiting in the town square for the results of local elections on hot June Saturday nights. History studies and government were naturally interesting and easy for me. No other subject particularly intrigued me. Politics and policy is my calling.

"Attending the unique program at the university (now called the Institute of Culture and Humanities) cofounded by Dr. James Hillman was an eye- and mind-opening experience. This course of study encouraged use of the imagination and image of the heart.

"Political consulting is seasonal work, and the season can last for three months to two years depending on the type of campaign—local, regional, or national," Hyde explains. "Political campaigning at a local level is extremely concentrated, normally three months, and is entered into by a candidate who has sometimes given very little serious thought about preparation of voter lists, coalition building, fund-raising, or issue presentation. The nature of the political candidate is usually one of tremendous energy and strong ego with an unshakable belief that the voting populace cannot live without his or her leadership. The consultant, on the other hand, must bring some order and consistent, coherent messages to the candidate and the workers. The atmosphere is one of chaotic, pressure-cooker days and nights.

"Everything is always late, unexpected, and includes last-minute and last-second decision making—sometimes like flipping a coin and forging ahead or backtracking. The days start as if the nights had never quit, and each workday lasts about eighteen hours. Both the candidate and campaign workers contract battle fatigue, which doesn't end until weeks after election day. Saturday and Sunday are not exempt.

"Each new campaign and candidate comes with the promise of a better day and a better way. It's exciting and hopeful to be involved in making a positive change by helping elect someone who can make a big difference. At least that's the upside. The downside is the exhaustion and condensed pressure of a compact campaign effort and, if such should occur, the loss of the candidate's best effort.

"I would advise others interested in entering this field to understand fully and honestly why you are working for a candidate. Know if you're primarily in it for a job, an appointment, the experience and excitement, or the candidate. Be realistic and don't hang around too long because burnout can set in quite soon. See *Wag the Dog* and *Primary Colors*—I found them to be pretty accurate campaign representations."

Meet K. Mark Takai, State Representative

K. Mark Takai earned a bachelor of arts degree in political science in 1990 and a master of public health degree in health education in 1993 from the University of Hawaii at Manoa in Honolulu. During his internship for his master of public health degree, he worked for a city council member for the city and county of Honolulu.

"My experiences at the University of Hawaii as an undergraduate student, graduate student, and employee probably attracted me to the state capitol," he says. "It was through these years that I had the most interaction with the legislators. I now serve as an elected state representative representing District 34, part of Aiea and part of Pearl City (both located near Pearl Harbor on Oahu).

"The idea of becoming an elected official interested me from the time I was a young boy (probably from fourth grade, when I was involved in student government). I continued to be involved with student government in high school serving as the student body president for a 2,400-student school and in college as the student body leader, representing more than 12,000 students. I truly enjoy all opportunities to interact with people from diverse backgrounds and interests.

"I declared my candidacy for public office in July 1994, won the primary election in September, and was declared the winner of the seat after the general election in November. The job of a state representative runs the gamut. There are probably three different 'jobs' of an elected official—very diverse but all very important. The first is my job as a community leader. This is probably the most rewarding part of being in public office. The interaction with the community—through the schools, community organizations, neighborhood board meetings, and so on—all provide me with the opportunity to listen and then respond to the desires and concerns of the public.

"This part of the job can also be very difficult. In the more than four years since first being elected, I have been very fortunate in that I have not had too many difficult meetings with the public; however, as a freeway project is currently being planned and the project calls for possible public condemnation of private property, I have had my fair share of angry constituents. Most times, though, I am able to work with the residents of our community to address their concerns.

"The second part of my job is as a lawmaker. Constitutionally, this is my most important responsibility. Seventy-five legislators decide which laws are passed.

"My third responsibility is as a politician (i.e., a political candidate). State House offices are up every two years, so since my first election in 1994, I have had to run two reelection campaigns. This is a very time-consuming process. The campaign season begins around July of even-numbered years and doesn't end until the general election in early November. Aside from raising money to run a successful campaign (marketing materials, brochures, advertisements, and so forth), the most difficult and time-consuming tasks of the political season are sign waving (waving to cars along the roadside in the mornings and afternoons) and door-to-door canvassing.

"A typical day for me depends on the time of year. During the legislative session (January to May), a typical day begins at 7:30 A.M. with a breakfast. Then it's off to the state capitol for committee meetings that begin at 8:30 or 9 A.M. We have private meetings in our offices or we catch up on phone calls before the House floor session at noon. Then it's time to eat lunch with constituents or go to a luncheon after the session. At 2 P.M. we start our committee hearings, which usually run until 7 P.M. After the committee hearings, I usually participate in community meetings, which usually run to 10 P.M.

"I usually keep Friday evenings free from office work and routinely spend that time with my wife. Saturdays are generally busy with committee hearings or community events. Sundays are typically days reserved for family activities.

"During the off-election year, nonsession months, I usually work in the office planning for upcoming events. As the state cochairperson of Hawaii's Children and Youth for the past three years and the state cochairperson of Hawaii's Junior Miss Scholarship Program for the past two years, I find myself sometimes even busier than during the legislative session.

"The period of nonsession months during the campaign season is really tough and grueling. And, including time spent at receptions, dinners, and so forth, I probably spend about seventy hours a week working. However, the people I work with (both in the state capitol and throughout the community) make my job most rewarding. I would not trade the experiences that I have had for any other job. Although it can be very stressful and time consuming, I truly enjoy my job as a state representative.

"I derive great pleasure from doing for others. For instance, one of my most rewarding moments occurred when I was able to provide assistance in getting funds to build a new traffic signal at an intersection that saw many near accidents, numerous accidents, and one fatality.

"The least enjoyable part of my job is knowing full well that every bill that we pass and that becomes law has a negative impact on someone or on a specific profession. Although I have voted for many bills that do much good for our community overall, sometimes it is these same bills that get people laid off from their jobs, and so forth. Knowing this causes me great pain.

"I would encourage anyone interested in pursuing this kind of career to talk to people about what their concerns are. Meet with various community leaders in your community. Get involved with political campaigns and volunteer or work for an elected official. If you are truly serious, begin your plans for an eventual run for public office. Good luck!"

For More Information

Information on appointed officials in local government can be obtained from:

International City/County Management Association
777 North Capitol Street NE, Suite 500
Washington, DC 20002.

Here are some additional resources:

Democratic National Committee
Young Democrats of America
430 South Capitol Street SE
Washington, DC 20003

Republican National Committee
310 First Street SE
Washington, DC 20003

The Congressional Management Foundation
513 Capitol Court NE, Suite 100
Washington, DC 20002

CHAPTER FIVE

Careers in Law

*No man is above the law and no man is below it; nor do we
ask any man's permission when we require him to obey it.*

THEODORE ROOSEVELT

HELP WANTED: LAWYER

Our well-known firm is seeking to hire another lawyer.
Candidates must have five years of experience and all of the
proper legal credentials to be practicing law in this state.
We seek someone who is personable, capable, empathetic,
and knowledgeable about both people and the law. Travel
will be a necessary part of the job, so we need someone who
can leave town on short notice when necessary. A future
partnership is definitely a possibility.

Law Careers

If you're considering a career as a lawyer, maybe you're holding
images of Johnny Cochran or the stars of TV's *Law and Order*
or *L.A. Law*. You probably remember *Perry Mason* or have seen
the show's reruns. His clients were always innocent, he always
got them off, and he always nabbed the real criminal.

But real life doesn't always follow the imagination of television
writers. If criminal law is the area that interests you, you should
know that many of your clients will not be innocent, and you
might not be able to get them all off. Some you'd even rather not
represent. But, in our justice system, everyone is innocent until

proven guilty, and everyone is entitled to legal defense. However, while criminal law is a very popular and much-publicized specialty, it is not the only avenue lawyers can pursue.

The more detailed aspects of a lawyer's job depend upon his or her field of specialization. Even though all lawyers are allowed to represent parties in court, some appear in court more frequently than others. Some lawyers specialize in trial work. These lawyers need an exceptional ability to think quickly and speak with ease and authority and must be thoroughly familiar with courtroom rules and strategy. But trial lawyers still spend most of their time outside the courtroom conducting research, interviewing clients and witnesses, and handling other details in preparation for trial.

Besides trial work, attorneys may specialize in other areas. Some may never see the inside of a courtroom. The majority of lawyers are in private practice, where they may concentrate on criminal or civil law.

Job Settings

Criminal Law

In criminal law, lawyers represent people who have been charged with crimes. Their responsibility is to argue their cases in courts of law. Criminal lawyers operate their own practices, work for private law firms, or represent clients under the auspices of the public defender's office.

For every F. Lee Bailey, there's a Marcia Clark, and for every Perry Mason, a Hamilton Burger (the prosecutor in the television series). Lawyers who work for state attorneys, general prosecutors, and courts play a key role in the criminal justice system.

At the federal level, attorneys investigate cases for the Department of Justice or other agencies. Also, lawyers at every government level help develop programs, draft laws, interpret legislation, establish enforcement procedures, and argue civil and criminal cases on behalf of the government.

Civil Law

In civil law, attorneys assist clients with litigation, wills, trusts, contracts, mortgages, titles, and leases. Some manage a person's property as trustee or, as executor, see that provisions of a client's will are carried out. Others handle only public interest cases, civil or criminal, that have a potential impact extending well beyond the individual client.

Other lawyers work for legal aid societies, private, nonprofit organizations established to serve disadvantaged people. These lawyers generally handle civil rather than criminal cases.

Some other specializations within civil law include:

bankruptcy

probate

international law

environmental law

intellectual property

insurance law

family law

corporate law

real estate law

house counsel

tax law

Lawyers are sometimes employed full-time by a single client. If the client is a corporation, the lawyer is known as house counsel and usually advises the company about legal questions that arise from its commercial or business activities. Such questions might relate to government regulations, patents, contracts with other companies, property interests, libel issues, or collective bargaining agreements with unions. Some of the entities that employ house counsel are banks and publishing houses.

Government Attorneys

Attorneys employed at the various levels of government make up still another category. The attorney general of any state is the chief law officer of the state. Below the attorney general, you will find hundreds of assistant attorneys, general or district attorneys, as they are often called, in offices in various cities throughout each state. They represent the state in civil actions, such as the big tobacco lawsuits that surface in the news from time to time.

In some states, the local prosecutors have an appellate division in each office, and these attorneys handle only appeals. They write briefs for the judges. Every once in a while, one side or the other will request an oral argument, and then the appeals attorneys will have to go to court. If the verdict is overturned, the state often has to retry the case.

Law Clerks

Law clerk is a misleading title. Many people mistakenly think it refers to someone who is an administrative assistant as opposed to an attorney. But law clerks are, indeed, full-fledged attorneys. A more fitting job title would be something along the lines of research attorney. Sometimes they're called elbow clerks because they work at the elbow of the judge, usually for a one- to two-year stint directly out of law school or, for some, as a full-time, professional career. Duties vary depending on the judge you work with, but often reading briefs, writing notes on them, and conducting research are a law clerk's main responsibilities.

In addition to a law degree, there are other qualifications you should have to qualify for this position. Most law clerks have graduated in at least the top quarter or higher of their class. As a full-time career, a job as a law clerk has its pluses and minuses.

Salaries are generally much lower than those paid by private law firms, and your job security depends on whether or not the judge you work for stays on the bench. He or she could retire or quit or fail to win reelection, and then you're out of a job. In contrast, your hours are more normal than busy firm lawyers, and there is usually less stress and competition to deal with.

Law Professors

A relatively small number of trained attorneys teach in law schools. Most are faculty members who specialize in one or more subjects. Others serve as administrators. Some work full-time in nonacademic settings and teach part-time.

Working Conditions

Lawyers spend most of their time in offices, law libraries, and courtrooms. Occasionally lawyers might meet with a client in his or her home or place of business and, when necessary, in a hospital or prison. They frequently travel to attend meetings; to gather evidence; and to appear before courts, legislative bodies, and other authorities.

Salaried lawyers in government and private corporations generally have structured work schedules. Lawyers in private practice may work irregular hours while conducting research, conferring with clients, or preparing briefs during nonoffice hours. Lawyers in private practice can often determine their own workloads.

Many specialties require that lawyers work long hours, and about half regularly work fifty hours or more per week. They are under particularly heavy pressure, for example, when a case is being tried. Preparation for court includes keeping abreast of the latest laws and judicial decisions.

Although legal work is generally not seasonal, the work of tax lawyers and other specialists may be an exception.

Responsibilities

No matter the setting, whether acting as advocate or prosecutor, all attorneys interpret the law and apply it to specific situations. This requires good research and communication abilities.

Lawyers perform in-depth research into the purposes behind the applicable laws and into judicial decisions that have been applied to those laws under circumstances similar to those currently faced by the client. While all lawyers continue to make use of law libraries to prepare cases, some supplement their searches of the conventional printed sources with computer software packages that automatically search the legal literature and identify legal texts that may be relevant to a specific subject. During litigation that involves many supporting documents, lawyers may use computers to organize and index the material.

Qualifications and Training

To practice law in the courts of any state or other jurisdiction, you must be licensed or admitted to its bar. Nearly all states require that applicants for admission to the bar pass a written bar examination. Most jurisdictions also require applicants to pass a separate written ethics examination.

Lawyers who have been admitted to the bar in one jurisdiction occasionally may be admitted to the bar in another without taking an examination if they meet that jurisdiction's standards of good moral character and have a specified period of legal experience. Federal courts and agencies set their own qualifications for those practicing before them.

To qualify for the bar examination in most states, an applicant must complete at least three years of college and graduate from a law school approved by the American Bar Association (ABA) or the proper state authorities.

Seven states accept the study of law in a law office or in combination with study in a law school; only California accepts the study of law by correspondence as qualifying for taking the bar examination.

Several states require registration and approval of students by the state Board of Law Examiners, either before they enter law school or during the early years of legal study. Most beginning lawyers then train with the government or experienced lawyers before they go out on their own. Some join established law firms and work very hard to become partners.

The required college and law school education usually takes seven years of full-time study after high school, four years of undergraduate study, followed by three years in law school. Although some law schools accept a very small number of students after three years of college, most require applicants to have a bachelor's degree.

To meet the needs of students who can attend only part-time, a number of law schools have night or part-time divisions that usually require four years of study. Typical courses for first-year law students include legal history, legal writing, and public speaking. Second- and third-year students typically take criminal law, contract law, corporate law, wills, and real estate law.

Acceptance by most law schools depends on the applicant's ability to show an aptitude for the study of law. This is usually demonstrated through good undergraduate grades and high scores on the Law School Admission Test (LSAT). All law schools approved by the ABA require that applicants take the LSAT. The quality of the applicant's undergraduate school, any prior work experience, and sometimes a personal interview are considered in the application review, but law schools vary in the weight that they place on each of these factors.

Graduates receive the degree of juris doctor (J.D.) or bachelor of laws (LL.B.) as the first professional degree. Advanced law degrees may be desirable for those planning to specialize, do research, or teach. Some law students pursue joint degree programs, which generally require an additional year. Joint degree programs are offered in a number of areas, including law and business administration and law and public administration.

Salaries for Lawyers

Law is a much more demanding profession than most people realize, and it is not always the high-income profession everyone thinks it is. Yes, there are a lot of attorneys out there earning a lot of money. But there are also attorneys running themselves ragged from courtroom to courtroom and barely earning enough to pay back their school loans.

Contrary to the experience of John Grisham's hero in *The Firm*, annual salaries for beginning lawyers in private industry average about $40,000. But, in some cases, top graduates from the nation's best law schools can start at more than $80,000 per year.

Factors affecting the salaries offered to new graduates include academic record; type, size, and location of the employer; and the specialized educational background desired.

Here's a look at average salaries for new law school graduates working in a variety of specializations:

Private Practice—$50,000

Business/Industry—$45,000

Higher Education—$35,000

Law Clerk—$35,000

Government—$34,500

Public Interest—$30,000

Salaries of experienced attorneys also vary widely according to the type, size, and location of their employers. The average salary of the most experienced lawyers in private industry is more than

$134,000, but some senior lawyers who are partners in the nation's top law firms earn more than $1 million annually.

General attorneys in the federal government average around $72,700 a year. The small number of patent attorneys working for the government average around $81,600.

Lawyers on salary receive increases as they assume greater responsibilities. Lawyers starting their own practices may need to work part-time in other occupations during the first years to supplement their incomes. Their incomes usually grow as their practices develop. Lawyers who are partners in law firms generally earn more than those who practice alone.

Words from the Pros

Meet Nicole D. Blake, Lawyer

Nicole Blake is a self-employed lawyer in Seattle, Washington. She received her bachelor of arts degree in political science from Loyola University in Chicago, then earned her juris doctorate from DePaul University in Chicago.

"I have been a lawyer since 1991," she says. "My first real job out of school was as a public defender. In that capacity, I became involved in dependency law, which is defending parents from losing their rights when the state has removed their kids and put them in foster care. But this was a difficult position because of the high caseload. Then I performed some nonlegal work as an adoption social worker for a nonprofit agency for a year and a half. Since I was the last one hired, I was laid off.

"In my private practice, I focus on dependency law, and that has naturally led to family law—divorce, adoption, and so forth. As a solo practitioner, I enjoy being my own boss and organizing my own schedule. Then again, I dislike organizing my own schedule and keeping my own books.

"I have always wanted to help others," says Blake. "I don't have a mathematical mind, but I do have a great ability and proclivity for argument, so it seemed an obvious career path. Also, I come from a family that stressed education. Several family members had already followed a career path in law. In fact, my cousin was one of the first blind lawyers admitted to practice in Chicago.

"I rarely know what any given day will really be like. Something unexpected happens every day. Certain responsibilities are constants, however. One activity that usually takes a huge chunk of my day is returning calls. I rarely answer the phone because this is one of the few ways that I can remain in charge of my own time. Another common responsibility is to attend hearings, often in more than one courthouse and more than one city at a time. Usually I work on at least one legal writing per day. Filing paperwork or figuring out what to do with any certain piece of paper is the time waster that I resent the most.

"I enjoy working with clients, particularly when things are working well. However, I like this aspect of my career less when clients don't understand my role or the abilities (and inabilities) of the law to deal with all of their life issues. Phone calls sometimes become oppressive because there are too many. Clients don't always know what is important, so I am swamped.

"I would advise individuals who are interested in getting into law to try debate teams in high school and college. Another bit of advice—study instead of going to parties so that you can get into one of the best possible law schools."

For More Information

The American Bar Association annually publishes *A Review of Legal Education in the United States,* which provides detailed information on each of the 177 law schools approved by the ABA, state requirements for admission to legal practice, a directory of state bar examination administrators, and other information on legal education. Single copies are free from the ABA, but there is a fee for multiple copies. Free information on the bar examination, financial aid for law students, and law as a career may also be obtained from:

Member Services
American Bar Association
541 North Fairbanks Court
Chicago, IL 60611

Association of American Law Schools
1201 Connecticut Avenue NW, Suite 800
Washington, DC 20036

Information on the LSAT, the Law School Data Assembly Service, applying to law school, and financial aid for law students may be obtained from:

Law School Admission Services
P.O. Box 40
Newtown, PA 18940

The specific requirements for admission to the bar in a particular state or other jurisdiction may also be obtained at the state capitol, from the clerk of the state Supreme Court, or from the administrator of the state Board of Bar Examiners.

CHAPTER SIX

Careers in Education

The foundation of every state is the education of its youth. DIOGENES

S killed teachers know that the more persuasive they are about the benefits of education, the more children will learn. So, it is their challenge to make learning interesting, challenging, and fun.

Educators Today

At the kindergarten and elementary school level, teachers play a crucial role in children's development because what children learn and are exposed to during their early years can shape their views, not only of themselves, but of the world at large. Kindergarten and elementary school teachers introduce children to language, numbers, science, and social studies. This can greatly affect later success or failure in school, work, and personal life.

At the elementary level, most teachers instruct one class of children in a variety of subjects. Sometimes two or three teachers work together or team teach. In other situations, a teacher may specialize in only one subject, such as art, music, science, reading, arithmetic, or physical education, or perhaps specialize in one area, such as special education.

In some areas, teachers act as facilitators or coaches, using interactive discussions and hands-on learning to help pupils learn and apply the concepts involved in subjects like English, mathematics, or science. As teachers move away from the more traditional, repetitive drill approaches and rote memorizing, they are more likely to use manipulatives and props to help children solve problems, understand abstract concepts, and develop critical thought processes. So, these days, instead of flash cards, teachers may be more apt to use board games, computers, science apparatus, or tape recorders.

Working in group settings in order to discuss and solve problems is becoming more and more common. In this way, students are being prepared for future workforce situations. To be prepared for the long run, students must be able to interact with others, adapt to new technology, and logically think through their problems. Teachers can encourage the development of these skills by providing these learning opportunities.

Secondary school teachers help students delve more deeply into the subjects already introduced in elementary school and also expose them to additional information about themselves and the world. Teachers at this level usually specialize in a particular subject, such as mathematics, biology, history, Spanish, theater, or English. In some cases, instructors may teach more than one subject or may be involved in related subjects such as American history, world history, and world geography.

At the college level, faculty members teach and advise students while studying, meeting with colleagues to keep up with developments in their fields, and consulting with government, business, nonprofit, and community organizations.

The Internet has provided a whole new world of opportunity for educators. Those with computer expertise may teach anything from individual classes on a wide variety of topics to regular college credit courses through a number of colleges and universities. It is even possible to earn college degrees on-line.

The Role of the Educator

Teachers at the elementary and high school levels prepare classroom presentations and also work with students on a one-to-one basis. They plan, evaluate, and assign lessons; prepare, administer, and grade tests; and listen to oral presentations by the students. They observe and evaluate students' performances and increasingly use new assessment methods, such as portfolios, which judge the student's overall progress at the end of a learning period. Additional assistance is then provided in the needed areas.

Teachers also grade papers, prepare report cards, and meet with parents and school staff to discuss individual problems and student progress (or lack thereof). Educators must also be adept at successfully maintaining classroom discipline.

In addition to classroom activities, some teachers oversee study halls and homeroom and supervise extracurricular activities. They identify physical or mental problems and refer students to the proper resource or agency for diagnosis and treatment. Secondary school teachers occasionally assist students in choosing courses, colleges, and careers. Teachers at all levels participate in educational conferences and workshops. In some school systems, teachers participate actively in management decisions regarding budgets, personnel, textbook choices, curriculum design, and teaching methods.

At the college level, teaching faculties are generally organized into departments or divisions, based upon subject or field. Professors often teach several different courses within their departments—English, composition, or fiction, for example. They may work with undergraduate or graduate students or both. Classes may be in the form of large lecture halls involving several hundred students, small seminars, or labs. Generally, professors are responsible for preparing lectures, exercises, and laboratory experiments; grading papers and exams; and advising individual students. Keeping abreast of developments in their field is an important aspect of their positions and, in most cases, educators are expected to experiment; collect and analyze data; examine original documents, literature, and other source material; develop hypotheses; arrive at conclusions; and publish their findings in scholarly journals, books, and electronic media.

Qualifications and Training

All fifty states and the District of Columbia require public elementary and high school teachers to be licensed. This is not required for teachers in private schools. Usually licensure is granted by the state Board of Education or a licensure advisory committee. Teachers may be licensed to teach the early childhood grades (usually nursery school through grade three); the elementary grades (grades one through six or eight); the middle grades (grades five through eight); a secondary education subject area (usually grades seven through twelve); or a special subject, such as reading or music (usually grades kindergarten through twelve).

Requirements for regular licenses vary by state. However, all require bachelor's degrees and completion of an approved teacher training program with a prescribed number of subject and education credits and supervised practice teaching. Some states require specific minimum grade point averages for teacher licensure. Others require teachers to obtain master's degrees in education, which involves at least one year of additional course work beyond the bachelor's degree with a specialization in a particular subject.

Almost all states require applicants for teacher licensure to be tested for competency in basic skills such as reading and writing, teaching skills, or subject master proficiency. Most states require continuing education for renewal of teaching licenses.

The National Council for Accreditation of Teacher Education currently accredits more than five hundred teacher education programs across the United States. Generally, four-year colleges require students to wait until the sophomore year before applying for admission to teacher education programs. Traditional education programs for kindergarten and elementary school teachers include courses designed specifically for those preparing to teach mathematics, physical science, social science, music, art, and literature, as well as prescribed professional education courses, such as philosophy of education, psychology of learning, and teaching methods. Aspiring secondary school teachers either major in the subjects they plan to teach while also taking education courses or major in education and take subject courses. Most programs require students to take computer classes and to perform student teaching.

Most college and university faculty fall into four academic categories: professor, associate professor, assistant professor, and instructor. These positions are usually considered to be tenure-track positions. Most faculty members are hired as instructors (often nontenure-track positions) or assistant professors. Educators need to serve a specified period—usually seven years—under term contracts. At the end of the contract period, their records of teaching, research, and overall contributions to the institutions are reviewed. Tenure is granted if the review is favorable. If denied tenure, they must leave the institution. Tenured professors cannot be fired without just cause and due process. This provides a large measure of protection for those who attain it.

Four-year colleges and universities generally only consider doctoral degree holders for full-time, tenure-track positions but may hire master's degree holders or doctoral candidates for certain disciplines, such as the arts, or for part-time and temporary jobs. In two-year colleges, master's degree holders often qualify for full-time positions. Doctoral programs, including time spent completing a master's degree and a dissertation, take an average of four to eight years of full-time study beyond the bachelor's degree. (A dissertation is a written report on original research in the candidate's major field of study. It sets forth an original hypothesis or proposes a model and tests it.)

No matter what subject area is involved, whether it be art, science, or air-conditioning repair, there are qualities and skills that all teachers must possess. In addition to being knowledgeable in their subjects, they must have the ability to communicate, inspire trust and confidence, and motivate students, as well as understand their educational and emotional needs. They should also be organized, dependable, and patient, as well as creative. Stamina, patience, commitment, and a sense of humor are also important. These are qualities that no degree can document.

At the college level, faculty members need to have inquiring and analytical minds and strong desires to pursue and disseminate knowledge. Additionally, they must be self-motivated and able to work in environments where they receive little direct supervision.

Working Conditions

Including the school duties that are performed outside the classroom, many teachers work more than forty hours per week. Most work the traditional ten-month school year with a two-month vacation during the summer. Those on the ten-month schedule may teach in summer sessions, take other jobs, travel, or pursue other personal interests. Many enroll in college courses or workshops to continue their educations. Teachers in districts with a year-round schedule typically work eight weeks, are then on vacation for one week, and have a five-week midwinter break.

At the elementary and high school levels, most states have tenure laws that prevent teachers from being fired without just cause and due process. Teachers may obtain tenure after they have satisfactorily completed a probationary period of teaching, normally three years. Tenure does not absolutely guarantee a job, but it does provide some security.

College faculty members generally have flexible schedules. Usually, they must be present for classes twelve to sixteen hours per week and also for faculty and committee meetings. In addition, most set up regular office hours for students to come to see them whenever necessary. The rest of their time is devoted to preparing for classes, grading papers and exams, studying, conducting research, supervising graduate students, and so forth.

Salaries

According to the National Education Association, the estimated average salary of all public elementary and secondary school teachers is about $40,000. The average takes into account new teachers just starting out and those who have been on the job as much as twenty years or more. Earnings will also vary depending on the area of the country. Private school teachers generally earn less than public school teachers. In some schools, teachers can earn extra pay for working with students in extracurricular activities, such as cheerleading or sports.

For teachers of higher education, earnings vary according to faculty rank and type of institution and, in some cases, by field. Faculty members in four-year institutions earn higher salaries, on the average, than those in two-year schools. In fact, those in two-year schools are often paid an hourly wage, which could range from $15 to $40 an hour.

According to a survey conducted by the American Association of University Professors, salaries for full-time faculty on nine-month contracts averaged more than $50,000 a year. Those on eleven- or twelve-month contracts earned more. Those just starting out could expect to earn approximately $20,000 to $30,000 a year, but salaries could be considerably less, depending upon the area of the country.

Most college and university faculty enjoy some unique benefits, including access to campus facilities, tuition waivers for dependents, housing and travel allowances, and paid sabbatical leaves. Part-time faculty generally enjoy fewer benefits than full-time faculty.

For adult education, earnings vary widely by subject, academic credentials, experience, and region of the country. Salaried adult education teachers who usually work full-time realize median earnings of approximately $29,000 a year. A new teacher might earn only in the teens. Part-timers are generally paid hourly wages and do not receive benefits or pay for preparation time outside of class.

The Job Hunt

Educators have a number of resources into which they can tap to help with their job searches.

College Career Placement Centers

Most colleges maintain career centers that receive regular job listings. They are posted on bulletin boards or housed in ring binders. You can also leave your resume on file there. Prospective employers often contact college career offices looking for likely candidates.

The Internet

This is an incredible source of information and particularly helpful to those who are job hunting. Use any of the search engines available to you and type in key words such as *employment, teaching,* and *jobs.* Your "hits" will include educational institutions, publications, and a wide variety of potential employers and job search services—most of which are available to you at no charge. Many newspapers also upload their classified sections to the Internet, and you can examine the help wanted ads in local newspapers or papers in the geographic location in which you'd prefer to work.

The Direct Approach

Contact school districts in desired areas to find out if they are interested in hiring new staff members. If not, find out if your application may be kept on file for future openings.

Newspaper Want Ads

Many school districts advertise their need for educators in newspapers. In particular, check the Sunday want ads.

The Chronicle of Higher Education

This is the old standby for those seeking positions within two- and four-year colleges and universities. It is a weekly publication available by subscription or in any library or college placement office.

Placement Agencies

For private schools particularly, both at home and abroad, placement agencies can provide a valuable source for finding employment. Some charge both the employer and the prospective employee a fee; others charge just one or the other.

Words from the Pros

Meet Michele Lyons Lefkovitz, Elementary Art Teacher

"I became an artist when someone handed me a box of crayons when I was in kindergarten at the age of four," says Michele Lyons Lefkovitz, elementary art teacher for Forest Glen Elementary School (an International Magnet Program) in Indianapolis, Indiana.

Lefkovitz attended the University of Cincinnati in the College of Design, Architecture, Art, and Community Planning. She earned bachelor's and master's degrees in education from the Herron School of Art (Indiana University). She is recognized as a Certified Arts and Crafts Teacher for the state of Indiana and has earned a Life License to teach kindergarten through twelfth grades.

"I began my career by teaching art to first through sixth graders in January 1976 at Lawrence Elementary School, filling in for a teacher who was on maternity leave," explains Lefkovitz. "I was there for one semester then taught at Crestview Elementary, also in Lawrence Township, for the next three and one half years. Upon the arrival of my children, I took a ten-year leave. I returned to the profession in the fall of 1990, when I took a position as a middle school art teacher in Pike Township. The first year, I taught at both Guion Creek Middle School and Lincoln Middle School. For the next three years, I taught exclusively at Lincoln Middle School. During those times, I taught art to sixth through eighth graders. This fall, I will begin my fifth year at Forest Glen Elementary.

"I have always loved the creative process of using the medium of art to express myself," says Lefkovitz. "Paint, crayons, markers, colored pencils, pen and ink, paper, scissors, glue, and pencils have been my companions for all these years. When I was young, I remember being so excited at Christmas because I just knew Santa would bring new art supplies!

"Color is one of my favorite elements of design. From an early age, I was very aware of color and all the many variations of each hue. When I was ready to attend college, I knew I wanted to go to art school. I just wasn't sure which area of art. I had considered commercial art and began as a design major. After two quarters of college, I decided to switch my major to art education. That combined my love of fine arts with my love for children. It has been a perfect combination for me. I still enjoy graphic design, and I have been the yearbook editor for eight years. Teaching art has been extremely rewarding, and I feel very fortunate in my chosen profession.

"I teach six forty-five-minute classes a day for a total of thirty classes a week. In the morning, I have bus duty. I am in charge of getting all 750 students to their classrooms. At the end of the day, I make sure they get on the correct buses. In between, I live in my classroom. Each day, I teach grades five, four, three, two, and one, in that order.

"Since I teach in an international school, our curriculum is driven by social studies. Each grade level studies a different continent. I teach art with a multicultural focus. My first graders learn about Latin America, second graders travel to Africa and Australia, third graders travel to Asia, fourth graders go to Europe and fifth graders study North America. Since the world is full of many cultures and art forms, I literally have the world at my fingertips. In my class, we are all individuals from many cultures, and we value diversity. I also make use of my extensive doll collection of international dolls to teach art forms and cultures.

"The world is a very colorful place and we make the most of it. Throughout the year, each child will draw, paint, create a clay piece, cut paper, and use crayon, marker, chalk, and colored pencils. Older children will use ink as well. The topics vary by age and grade, but they all share the same mediums. Each session, I spend about five minutes giving instructions to each class and allow a five-minute cleanup. In between, we create and enjoy! The days are very busy and full. My class is only quiet during instruction and dismissal. Otherwise, we are all learning and sharing. I never sit down and am never bored. After school, I attend meetings. In total, I spend about forty plus hours a week at school.

"I love the relationships I have with my students and their families. As an art teacher, I have the same students for all five years of elementary school. So I get to really know them well. I am allowed to see them mature and grow up.

"I love art and feel that my students learn to share my enthusiasm. Many of them say art is their favorite subject. They have a sense of freedom and expression in my classroom. I emphasize that there is no one way to do anything. The creative process is very important because it involves genuine thinking skills.

"I would highly recommend the field of art education. However, it's important to know that there are considerably fewer art teachers in a school system than there are regular classroom teachers. In fact, some schools don't even have an art teacher. Thus, the principle of supply and demand comes into play. So I would suggest that perhaps a person have a second area of study as a backup. Most important—I would recommend that you follow your dreams, and if you choose what you love to do, you will be happy."

Meet Louise Tenbrook Whiting, Instructor/Trainer

Louise Tenbrook Whiting earned a master of arts degree in counseling psychology from Sierra University in Santa Monica, California. She is self-employed as an instructor/trainer.

"I was a member of a songwriters' organization in Southern California and taught some music classes," she says. "Although I was providing a needed service, I knew there was something lacking for me. Later, I became employed as a program manager for a crisis intervention/suicide prevention hot line. I not only managed the office, I became one of the trainers for our volunteer staff. Through this experience, I learned that I enjoyed helping others with problems and found it rewarding to train others to do the same. So while I was there, I decided to return to college and change my major from religion to counseling psychology. I have been involved in the teaching and training of communication and interpersonal skills ever since. I was challenged to pursue a new dream for my life.

"Today, I am self-employed and work alone in my home office. I am in a stress-free environment where I am able to set my own schedule and make changes as desired. When I have an outside appointment, I simply adjust my schedule. If I choose to work late or in the middle of the night, I have that option. When I decide to take time off, I am able to do so—within reason of course.

"The majority of my teaching is done on-line. I teach classes on speaking skills, communication, and interpersonal skills. I am using my education, former employment, and life experience to develop my classes and write the course materials needed. Most of the classes are self-study. One on-line class, called Own Your Own Life, has weekly meetings. In this class, I teach interpersonal and life skills to former victims of abuse.

"What I like most about the classes I teach in person is being able to personally interact with each student and observe facial expressions and body language. I love to use humor—this works in person, yet does not translate well on-line. I am a performer at heart, and being in front of an audience, students or otherwise, is great! My income comes from different sources, which indicates that my work offers variety. However, the downside is that my income varies from month to month, and there is frequently a time lapse in receiving it.

"What I like the least regarding teaching in person is the fact that the days are usually long and exhausting. And sometimes I am slightly anxious at first. But then I am soon in my element and on a roll. The downsides? Minimal.

"Although I prefer working alone, having someone else around tends to create more energy. Also, when I am busy, which I am much of the time, I tend to isolate myself too much and not get out as I should. I also neglect eating regular meals—or forget to eat at all. I often feel glued to the computer and to my work. The majority of the time I am self-motivated. When I am not, I can easily waste time.

"The advice I would give to others is to determine what your interest or your passion is and learn what education or skills you need to acquire before pursuing your dream, then follow through with what you have learned you must do, discipline yourself to achieve your dream (no matter what the challenges are or who tries to dissuade you), and never give up.

"Following a recent class I taught, I received an E-mail from one of the students. Here is a quote from that E-mail: 'You are the first person in my entire thirty years who has ever stood up in front of me and made any sense to me at all. I would not change this day in class for anything. I feel that I learned more from being there than from any other day in my entire life.' This makes the job worth every minute of it."

Meet David Mecozzi, Teacher

David Mecozzi earned his bachelor of science degree in business administration from California State University at Northridge. He earned his teacher's credential at the University of Redlands in California. Currently, he is employed by the Etiwanda School District as a fifth grade teacher at West Heritage Elementary School in Fontana, California.

"Previously, I spent ten years in the business world," Mecozzi says. "The last five were with IBM Corporation. I took one of IBM's severance packages to pursue a career in teaching because I wanted to have a career that would make a difference in society. I was, and continue to be, concerned about the adult role models our future—the kids—have. So, instead of just griping about it, I looked into careers that would satisfy that concern. Teaching jumped out at me. Coaching Little League baseball, I believe, made me start thinking that I really wanted to work with children.

"I was also attracted to the schedule. Having missed much of my son's infancy due to business trips, long, odd hours, and such, the schedule a teacher keeps (or so it seemed on paper) really appealed to me.

"Now the reality. A typical teacher's day is extremely hectic. There are literally thousands of interruptions that need to be handled daily. I'm not making that up; there have been actual studies done. I am responsible for instructing the children in six different subjects and ensuring that they meet grade-level standards. I need to develop lessons that are engaging because a teacher's challenge is to create lessons that make the students want to do them even though many children don't even want to be at school!

"Educators also need to deal with administrative needs and paperwork. This can be frustrating and saps a lot of energy and time away from what a teacher is supposed to do. Another outside variable a teacher deals with are parents. Just last year alone, I changed my way of doing things several times to meet and satisfy legitimate parental requests. That's not counting the time spent stressing over the not-so-legitimate requests.

"Teachers are expected to be experts at everything. The students view us as some kind of all-knowing being. I spend the first few weeks of each school year working to change that image. What a difference it makes for the kids to see that even the teacher makes mistakes and doesn't fall apart, or the world doesn't end! Learning then takes place because the kids feel freer to try.

"The hours a teacher works are very misleading. Most people think teachers have 'cushy' jobs. Everybody wants a job where they can go to work at 8 A.M. and leave at 3 P.M., right? And let's not talk about the summer! (And they get to work with kids—how hard can that be?)

"Now here's the actual scoop: I get to work at 7:30 A.M. The kids come into the classroom at 8 A.M. and leave at 2:30 P.M. Between 2:30 P.M. and 4:30 P.M., I clean my room, eat lunch (I work through lunch), grade papers, prepare for the next day, attend grade-level committee meetings, and so forth. By contract, I am obligated to stay until 3 P.M. The time I actually leave is around 4:30 P.M. Since I pick up my own kids from school and the sitter, that is the time I have to leave. And I am not alone; there are teachers who don't leave the school site until 6:30 P.M. every day, including Friday.

"During the heart of the school year, I can be found awake late at night thinking of how to reach the kids or how to present something in a different manner. I rarely get a full night's sleep from September through June.

"To me, the greatest reward of teaching is having a positive effect on a child's life. I have received several letters from former students who have told me that they are doing well in school because they listened to me. I can't recall one time in the business world that I experienced the warm feeling I felt after reading those letters.

"I enjoy being able to 'perform' in front of kids, and making them laugh brings me much happiness. I enjoy the 'aha' moments when the kids learn something for the first time. I enjoy how the job lets my creativity flow. On the other hand, I am dismayed by children who have little or no motivation to learn and are bent on taking my time away from those students who do. Nothing is more frustrating to a teacher than to watch a child choose not to grow.

"I take issue with the apparent lack of respect toward the teaching profession. Hardly a day goes by that I don't read in the newspaper about someone blaming teachers for all of society's woes. This profession suffers because everyone thinks that they could be teachers. Many think, 'It can't be that hard—they have teachers' editions that tell you exactly what to say!' My advice would be:

1. Get into teaching *only* if you want to help children develop into successful adults. Any other reason will not a good teacher make. If you're in it only for the schedule, you won't put in the time required to be an effective teacher. You, the profession, and, most importantly, the kids will suffer.

2. Do what's right for the students first, then yourself second. If teaching that social studies lesson would really help the students, even though you'd rather keep on with math— switch to social studies. If sending work folders home weekly makes parents happy, though it's more work for you, do it.

3. Find a mentor. It doesn't have to be one assigned to you by your district. Find a helpful person on campus you can go to

and talk things over with, commiserate with, and so forth. Very helpful. This helped get me through my first year.

4. Never be a reason people say your profession is not really a profession. Dress and act professionally. Treat all with equal respect.

5. Never forget that, whether you like it or not, you *are* a role model. A major part of this job is being a role model. If you don't want to be one, don't enter the profession.

6. Never forget that you are not the students' friend; you are their teacher—a far greater role in their lives. If you try to be their friend, you are not only letting your profession down but your students as well.

7. Be consistent and fair. When you make a rule, don't waver. Stick to it. If the students feel it's unfair, listen. If it is, change it. But if it is fair, don't. Remember rule number six on this one. Sometimes you will be very unpopular, but the kids will thank you for it (not all of them, but most will). And, in the long run, you are performing a greater service."

For More Information

Information on teachers' unions and education-related issues may be obtained from:

American Federation of Teachers
555 New Jersey Avenue NW
Washington, DC 20001

National Education Association
1201 Sixteenth Street NW
Washington, DC 20036

A list of institutions with teacher education programs accredited by the National Council for Accreditation of Teacher Education can be obtained from:

National Council for Accreditation of Teacher Education
2010 Massachusetts Avenue NW, Second Floor
Washington, DC 20036

For information on voluntary teacher certification requirements, contact:

National Board for Professional Teaching Standards
300 River Place
Detroit, MI 48207

A list of institutions offering training programs in special education may be obtained from:

Council for Exceptional Children
1920 Association Drive
Reston, VA 22091

For additional information contact:

American Association for Adult and Continuing Education
1101 Connecticut Avenue NW, Suite 700
Washington, DC 20036

American Association for Higher Education
One Dupont Circle NW, Suite 360
Washington, DC 20036

American Association of Christian Schools
P.O. Box 2189
Independence, MO 64055

American Association of Colleges for Teacher Education
One Dupont Circle NW, Suite 610
Washington, DC 20036

American Association of State Colleges and Universities
One Dupont Circle NW, Suite 700
Washington, DC 20036

Association for Childhood Education International
11141 Georgia Avenue, Suite 200
Wheaton, MD 20902

Council for American Private Education
One Massachusetts Avenue NW, Suite 700
Washington, DC 20001

National Association for the Education of Young Children
1834 Connecticut Avenue NW
Washington, DC 20009

National Association of Independent Schools
75 Federal Street
Boston, MA 02110

About the Author

J an Goldberg's love for the printed page began well before her second birthday. Regular visits to the book bindery where her grandfather worked produced a magic combination of sights and smells that she carries with her to this day.

Childhood was filled with composing poems and stories, reading books, and playing library. Elementary and high school included an assortment of contributions to school newspapers. While a full-time college student, Goldberg wrote extensively as part of her job responsibilities in the College of Business Administration at Roosevelt University in Chicago. After receiving a degree in elementary education, she was able to extend her love of reading and writing to her students.

Goldberg has written extensively in the occupations area for General Learning Corporation's *Career World Magazine*, as well as for the many career publications produced by CASS Communications. She has also contributed to a number of projects for educational publishers including Capstone Publishing, Publications International, Scott Foresman, Addison-Wesley, and Camp Fire Boys and Girls. She is coauthor of the revised and updated edition of *Perfectionism: What's Bad About Being Too Good?*

As a feature writer, Goldberg's work has appeared in *Parenting Magazine*, *Today's Chicago Woman*, *Opportunity Magazine*, *Chicago Parent*, *Correspondent*, *Opportunity Magazine*, *Successful Student*, *Complete Woman*, *North Shore Magazine*, and the Pioneer Press newspapers. In all, she has published more than 350 pieces as a full-time freelance writer.

In addition to *Careers for Persuasive Types and Others Who Won't Take No for an Answer*, she is the author of *Careers for Scientific Types and Others with Inquiring Minds*, *Careers for*

*Patriotic Types and Others Who Wish to Serve Their Country,
Careers for Class Clowns and Other Engaging Types, Careers
for Color Connoisseurs and Other Visual Types, Careers for
Competitive Spirits and Other Peak Performers, On the Job:
Real People Working in Communications, On the Job: Real Peo-
ple Working in Entertainment, Great Jobs for Music Majors,
Great Jobs for Theater Majors, Great Jobs for Computer Sci-
ence Majors, Careers for Courageous People, Careers in Jour-
nalism, Great Jobs for Accounting Majors, On the Job: Real
People Working in Science, Opportunities in Research and
Development Careers, Opportunities in Entertainment Careers,*
and *Opportunities in Horticulture Careers,* all published by
NTC/Contemporary Publishing Group, Inc.